I SEE A VOICE

Michael Rosen

STANLEY THORNES (PUBLISHERS) LTD

Acknowledgements to the following for permission to use photographs:

Pages 9, 15, 51, 56, 75, 81 Barnaby's Picture Library; pages 18, 58, 63 Mary Evans Picture Library; page 30 Margaret Bourke-White/Life Magazine-Time Inc; page 35 Chris Davies, Report; page 79 London Borough of Tower Hamlets; page 85 Kobal Collection; page 90, 94 Imperial War Museum; page 61 Collins Publishers for artwork from *The Machine Breakers*.

Acknowledgements to the following for permission to use copyright material:

Roger McGough for *Nooligan* from *In the Glassroom* (Jonathan Cape); Grove Press Inc, New York for *When the Indians* from *A Child's Garden of Verses for the Revolution;* Vista Books, London for *In this City* from *Jazz Poems* ed. Anselm Hollo; Edward Braithwaite for *Limbo* from *The Arrivants* (Oxford University Press); Adrian Mitchell for *A Child is Singing* from *Poems* (Jonathan Cape), and *Back in the Playground Blues* (unpublished); Gouveia de Lemos for *Song of Agony* from *When Bullets Began to Fly* ed. Dickinson (East Africa Publishing House); Collett Dickenson Pearce & Partners for *Wrangler Jeans;* Frankie Armstrong for *We Must Choose;* Peggy Seeger and Harmony Music for *I'm Gonna be an Engineer;* Georgia Garrett for *Manwatching;* Adrian Henri for *Love is... from Tonight at Noon* (Rapp & Whiting); Liz Hutchins for *She Said;* Faber & Faber for *The General* by Siegfried Sassoon; Tom Paxton and Harmony Music for *What Did You Learn In School Today?* Linton Kwesi Johnson for *It Dread inna Inglan;* Liz Lochhead for *After Leaving the Castle* from *The Grimm Sisters* (Next Editions in association with Faber & Faber); Adrian Mitchell for *Requirements in the Shelter;* Northern Songs for *Imagine* by John Lennon; Joanne Edwards for *Birkenhead;* Eyre Methuen for *Questions from a Worker Who Reads* by Bertholt Brecht trans. Michael Hamburger; Danny Marriott for *The Old Warehouse* and *Chainman;* John Pole for *Centre Point;* Ian Milner/George Theiner for translation of *Five Minutes After the Air Raid* by Miroslav Holub (Penguin Modern European Poets); Jonathan Cape for *Naming of Parts* from *A Map of Verona* by Henry Reed; Alan Ross for *Survivors* from *Open Sea* (London Magazine Editions), and *Night Patrol* from *Poems 1942-67* (Eyre & Spottiswoode); Marie J Douglas for *Vergissmeinicht* from *Selected Poems* (Faber & Faber); James Kirkup for *No More Hiroshimas* from *Refusal to Conform* (Oxford University Press).

Whilst every effort has been made to trace ownership of copyright, the publishers would be grateful to hear from copyright holders whom we have been unable to contact.

Originally published in 1981 by Hutchinson Education
Reprinted 1982, 1983, 1984, 1987 (twice)

Reprinted in 1989 by
Stanley Thornes (Publishers) Ltd
Old Station Drive
Leckhampton
CHELTENHAM GL53 0DN

Reprinted 1990

ISBN 0 7487 0187 7

Designed by Intem Design Associates
Printed and bound in Great Britain at
The Bath Press, Avon.

CONTENTS

Cover Picture: 'A child is singing' by Abiola Agana (Age 7), Streatham Wells Primary School, London, based on the poem by Adrian Mitchell on page 22.

PREFACE

Some people have spent many years of their lives worrying. And, believe it or not, what they worried about was *What is poetry?*

Of course, if you don't ask yourself the question, you won't have the worries. This book is about poetry but I'll try not to make you worried about poetry or even worse make you worry about *what it is*. I've given myself a different job: arranging a 'meeting' between *you* and some people who try and

talk to you,
write to you,
write *for* you –
maybe even
write *about* you.

After you've heard these people, what they've got to say – a little about *why* they said it – you can take it or leave it. No one writing this book thinks poetry is Medicine – that is to say 'you may not like it but it's good for you'.

After reading it, I hope that you'll feel able to do two things more confidently – write poems about things that interest you and write *about* poems that interest you.

INTRODUCTION

Roses are red
Violets are blue
Most poems rhyme
This one doesn't.

TRADITIONAL

On the strength of each link of the cable
Depends the might of the chain
Who knows when you may be tested
So live as if you bear the strain.

ANONYMOUS

School taught me
to write my name
to recite the answers
to feel ashamed
to stand in corners
to wait in line
to kiss the rod
to be on time
and trust in God
To make me a model citizen
That was their goal
Well I don't know about that
But it was useful training
For a career on the dole.

LEON ROSSELSON

As thro' this world I ramble
I see lots of funny men
Some will rob you with a six-gun
And some with a fountain pen.

WOODY GUTHRIE

Chips!
Lovely and greasy
You chuck the salt and vinegar on
Gobble 'em all up
Nice!

SCHOOL PUPIL

creepy crawly custard
green snot pie
all mashed up with a dead dog's eye
slugs and bogies spread on thick
all washed down
with a cup of cold sick.

CHILDREN'S TRADITIONAL RHYME

When I was young, I used to be
As fine a lad as ever you'd see,
Till the Prince of Wales he said to me
'Come and join the British army'.
Too ra loo ra loo ra loo
They're looking for monkeys up in the zoo –
And if I had a face like you –
I'd join the British army.

TRADITIONAL

Did you laugh? Did you think? Did they please you? Did you go back and read any of them again? I hope so. Did you read any of them to anyone else? I chose them in the hope that you would.

A poem is written by someone.

Poets are comedians, teachers, smarty pants, show-offs, nags, hecklers, gassers, frauds, actors, conjurors, mimics, orators, conversationalists, teasers, thinkers.

Poems are constructed, selected, performed, screamed, told, whispered, sung, described, witnessed, seen, felt, overheard.

A poem says something.

Poems are jokes, lessons, games, speeches, complaints, boasts, hopes, dreams, rumours, insults, gossip, memories, lists.

I see each poem I write
    each poem I read
    each poem I hear
as part of a conversation, a chat. When you meet someone and he or she says something to you, they expect you to react – do something. It's the same with a poem – answer back, laugh, cry, tell a story, run away or call him or her a liar.

People disagree about very important things. Things like money, sex, race, bombs, school, home, parents, work, police, clothes, humour and music. We may also agree with each other but we won't know unless we discuss it or argue it out. Poems are ways of beginning such arguments.

RESPONDING TO POEMS

Broadly speaking, there are two roads you can go up after hearing or reading a poem. One is creative – *'Have a go yourself'*. The other is critical – *'Look again closely'*.

Road One – Have a go yourself

Everyone can have a go.
Everyone can answer a poem.
Everyone can talk about –
or write about –
a dream they've had
a favourite food
an accident
a game
something that annoys them
a street scene
a memory
a lost object
a meeting
a goodbye
a friend
a cruel thing
a trick
a good laugh
an unfair thing
a conversation
a fear
a good time
a hope

ACTIVITY

1. Choose any one of the poems at the start of this book. Write a short poem in the same style as a reply to the one you've chosen.
2. Write a poem to share with your class. Take one of the topics from the 'Have a go yourself' list.

   Think of a situation in which you were involved with that topic in some way.

   Jot down in words, phrases, and whole sentences as much as you can remember and how you feel (or felt) about it.

   Then use these words as 'raw material' to make a poem about the topic.

   Add any other words you need and make other changes to improve it.

   Use the poems at the start of this chapter to help you choose a style and layout.
3. Choose any of the poems at the start. What kind of argument is it starting? Who with? Do you agree or disagree with it?
4. Write a short poem that opens up a conversation about one of the topics on page 7.

Road Two – Look again closely

Here is an Instruction Manual on how to 'look again closely'. I'm going to use Roger McGough's poem *Nooligan* as an example.

NOOLIGAN

I'm a nooligan
dont give a toss
in our class
I'm the boss
(well, one of them)

I'm a nooligan
got a nard 'ead
step out of line
and youre dead
(well, bleedin)

I'm a nooligan
I spray me name
all over town
footballs me game
(well, watchin)

I'm a nooligan
violence is fun
gonna be a nassassin
or a nired gun
(well, a soldier)

ROGER MCGOUGH

1.   Theme. The general meaning. What ideas and feelings is this person trying to say to us?

Roger McGough mocks the kind of boy who thinks he's big, who says all kinds of things to make himself sound bigger than everybody else. He is trying to say how pathetic it is that some boys have to go about boasting how violent they are.

2.   *Development of the theme. A poet seems to tell us his or her ideas and feelings step by step, moment by moment, one event after another. Can you describe these steps?*

In *Nooligan* the steps are easy to see, because they are the four verses. Each verse is a new boast. But also, each verse has a last line which is what the nooligan says to himself. Each of his boasts is shown to be empty because the last line of each verse tells us what he's really like.

Step one   He tells us he's the boss. He then admits he's only 'one of them', which is a daft thing to say because you can't have more than one boss!

Step two   He threatens us. He tells us if we do anything wrong, he'll kill us. He then admits he won't *quite* kill us – which probably means he won't even touch us.

Step three   He tells us he's round the town with his spray can, full of football mania. He then admits he doesn't actually *play* football.

Step four   He tells us about his aim and purpose in life: to make his violence into a job – to be paid to be violent. He then admits he won't be an assassin, but simply 'a soldier'.

I take this last sentence to be slightly different from the last sentences in the other three verses. This time Roger McGough seems to be saying that this kind of boy, going about with these kind of mad boasts in his head, might also be the kind of boy who recruits for the Army.

Can you guess what step is coming next as you listen?

One step we learn to expect is the last line of each verse – the giveaway line that shows up the nooligan for what he really is. It is the 'regular form', the pattern of the poem, that leads us to expect the last line to come each time.

Can you describe how you feel as you make each step?

Step one   First of all I thought this was going to be about someone who talked big – and maybe *was* big: a kind of back street Muhammed Ali. Then, with the last line of the verse, I realised this was a poem which was going to show this nooligan to be all mouth. I laughed.

Step two   I now know the shape of the poem. 'I'm a nooligan' is like a chorus. I can feel the picture of the nooligan growing in front of me. I can see that he has two voices: public (to us), private (under his breath, to himself). I begin to recognise the nooligan in boys I know. I am glad this poem ridicules them, because I don't like boys like this.

Step three This time I like the way Roger McGough seems to say that people who shout the most about football sometimes don't even play themselves. All talk – no doing.

Step four Suddenly, I stop laughing. This verse is still mocking the nooligan, but seems very serious. I find it quite worrying and I wonder if McGough is right. Do boys like this join the Army? Maybe he is saying that all soldiers are nooligans, paid nooligans, or that being a nooligan is a kind of training-ground for being a soldier.

3. Voices. Poets are mimics and ventriloquists. Write down a few words to describe the voices in the poems.

There are two voices: public Nooligan and private Nooligan. The poet is mimicking the football fan, loudmouth, bully, who is in himself an all-talk – no-do lad.

Say whether you were tricked, amused, surprised, offended by any of these voices.

I was amused and surprised by the way the nooligan shows himself up – the one voice showing how empty the other voice is.

4. The situation. Why did the poet choose to say that?

I think Roger McGough wanted to say several things here. I think he doesn't like the violent talk of some boys he hears and I don't think he likes the idea that maybe it's this kind of violent talk and boasting that leads some lads into wanting to be soldiers.

Does it matter?

I think this matters a lot. In a very enjoyable funny way, Roger McGough has said some quite serious things about certain kinds of persons we see about us, in schools, in football stadiums or maybe in uniform. I think it is a very powerful statement against the kind of people who look at vandal-ism and say – 'What they need is a spell in the Army'. In one way McGough is saying all *that* would do would be giving them the chance to carry on being a Nooligan, legally: turning illegal violence into legal viol-ence. That's an idea worth thinking about.

ACTIVITY

Write about how one of these poems develops ideas, feelings and situation.

WHEN THE INDIANS

When the Indians
Sold
New York
For a handsome
Sum of
Glass beads,
They scouted west
And crossed
What is now called
The Mississipi,
Travelling west
On what is now called
Route 66
Until they arrived at
What is now called
California.
They decided to
Sell this too
For what is now
Called money,
But the whites
Took it with
What is now called
Guns.

WILLIAM EASTLAKE

IN THIS CITY

In this city, perhaps a street.
In this street, perhaps a house.
In this house, perhaps a room.
And in this room a woman sitting,
Sitting in the darkness, sitting and crying
For someone who has just gone through the door
And who has just switched off the light
Forgetting she was there.

ALAN BROWNJOHN

Style

A poet wants you to listen. Here are some of the tools that poets use to encourage that:

1 rhythm
2 rhyme
3 alliteration
4 repetition
5 metaphor and simile
6 juxtaposition of images
7 punning
8 voices and tone of voice
9 atmosphere and mood
10 pattern
11 emphasis and surprise, breaking the pattern

Anything you know of as a poem will use some of these techniques and many other ways of saying things too. When you come to writing or talking *about* poems, looking closely at them, you may find it handy

(i) to know how to recognise these techniques
(ii) to point them out
(iii) to say whether they help you to listen to what the poet is trying to say
  – if so, why? if not, why not?

1 Rhythm

Everything we say, sing or chant has rhythm. Just say your name over and over again and that makes a rhythm. Listen to football crowds, worksongs, skipping rhymes.

Come on you Re - eds
Come on you Re - eds

What a load of rubbish

Eng - gland; Eng - gland

Take this hammer - wah!
Carry it to the captain – wah!
Take this hammer – wah!
Carry it to the captain – wah!

All-in-together girls
It's fine weather girls . . .

I don't want to say anything too obvious about rhythm. Anyone who has banged a drum, tapped their feet to a bit of music, joined in a chant, doesn't need to be told that strong clear rhythms seem to be very attractive to us all. Poetry is a way of making people sit up and take notice of *this* word rather than *that* one; this group of words rather than another group of words. Every word has a meaning, it is an idea. So poetry is a way of making people sit up and take notice of an idea. Here is an example.

Do you know what limbo-dancing is?

The drums beat a rhythm and the dancer moves to the rhythm and performs the amazing feat of going under a lower and lower bar in time to the rhythm.

That's a boring way of describing something very exciting! Now, a group of people invented this way of dancing at some point in their history. Suppose you want to tell other people about it in almost the same way as they dance it – you write a history-of-limbo limbo dance-poem!

LIMBO

And limbo stick is the silence in front of me
limbo

limbo
limbo like me
limbo
limbo like me

long dark night is the silence in front of me
limbo
limbo like me
stick hit sound
and the ship like it ready

stick hit sound
and the dark still steady

limbo
limbo like me

long dark deck and the water surrounding me
long dark deck and the silence is over me

limbo
limbo like me
stick is the whip
and the dark deck is slavery

stick is the whip
and the dark deck is slavery

limbo
limbo like me
drum stick knocks
and the darkness is over me

knees spread wide
and the water is hiding me

limbo
limbo like me

knees spread wide
and the dark ground is under me

down
down
down

and the drummer is calling me
limbo
limbo like me

sun coming up
and the drummers are praising me

out of the dark
and the dumb gods are raising me

up
up
up
and the music is saving me

hot
slow
step
on the limbo ground

EDWARD BRATHWAITE

Here you have an idea about limbo dance and you have a limbo dance rhythm. The rhythm of the words draws our attention to what Edward Brathwaite wants to tell us. Before I read this poem I thought limbo dancing was something to do with shows put on for tourists in Jamaica! Suddenly Edward Brathwaite has thrown slavery and limbo together, linked one idea (limbo) to another idea (slavery) with *rhythm*.

It made me think about what I know about slavery, that could possibly be anything to do with people bending over backwards very, very low off the ground.

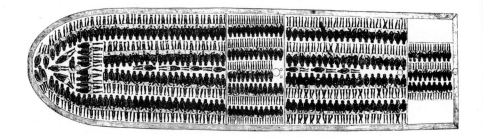

When the British and Portuguese slave-merchants took Africans across the Atlantic Ocean to America and the Caribbean Islands, they chained the African people, lying down on their backs in the dark, below deck. Many died. Some survived this terrible ordeal – they managed to keep fit.

How?

Limbo.

I've had to change the picture in my mind of limbo as a tourist stunt. A poem is a new way of looking at an idea. The rhythm of a poem can take us to the idea, can link one idea to another.

2   Rhyme

I know an old bloke
his name is Lord Jim
He had a wife
who threw tomatoes at him.

Now tomatoes are juicy –
and don't injure the skin
But these ones they did
They was inside a tin.

TRADITIONAL

These lines have rhyming words – *Jim* and *him*, *skin* and *tin*.

I think the writer wants us to have a laugh. Anyone who tells a joke knows it's no use telling a joke where the laugh comes half-way through a word or sentence – it has to come at the end of the sentence. The great thing about rhyme is that it can bring our attention round to the words that'll make us laugh. The gag about Lord Jim's wife throwing tomatoes comes right at the end, when we hear it's the tin.

Sometimes rhyming is a very mechanical thing, but other times a writer uses it to grab our attention and almost *force* us to listen. It may also be used to emphasise key words in a more serious poem.

There is another point here: it's to do with *memory* and *predictability*. If I want you to remember an idea, a story or an account of something then if I make it rhyme, and give it a regular rhyme, then the chances are, you'll find it easier to remember. And with a bit of luck, if you find it easier to remember, you'll find it easier to *re-tell*. And what could a writer, poet, or performer want more, than for someone to be able to read her or his poem and then be able to go off and perform it themselves.

3 *Alliteration*

Do you know any tongue-twisters? They are examples of alliteration gone mad: taking words with the same consonants and linking them together to make some sort of sense, but almost impossible to say.

She sells sea-shells on the sea-shore
She shells she-shells on the see-saw
She sells sea-sells . . .
Oh, I give up!

You might well be told that this isn't poetry. But if poetry is a way of using meanings of words, sounds of words and rhythms of words, then I'd have thought tongue-twisters are very good examples of these.

The other great use of alliteration is linking. If you give someone a nick-name you want everyone to remember it and use it eg; Cheerful Charlie, Dirty Dick, Big Bill, etc. Alliteration links one word to another and so links one idea to another. A poet may want to do that for various reasons; eg to surprise us, give us a laugh, soothe us, make music.

Advertisers love using it too, to make their products seem more desirable or their qualities more memorable. I remember once a local ironmongers trying to sell off some old coal-bunkers he had wanted to get rid of as: *Britain's Biggest Bunker Bargain!*

People who write poems and people who write about poems often talk about hard and soft sounds. For example, *b d k gg* are thought to be hard and *ss sh f l p* soft. So some writers like to say that when a poet uses consonants from the hard group this hammers the meaning home or lends a brutality to the meaning. Alternatively, if the alliteration comes from the soft group this soothes us, makes the poem musical, melodic, sweeter, etc. I should beware of this. *b* is for *beautiful*; *d* is for *dove*; snakes *hiss*; Rice Krispies *snap* and *pop*.

Rather than suggest that any given consonant is hard or soft as a reason why a poet might choose to be alliterative with it, I like to think more in terms of linking, the association of ideas, joining one word to another so that they stick together in *your* mind in the way they have come to stick together in the *poet's* mind, whether it be, for instance, about
   (i) the dawn 'massing in the east her melancholy army' (Wilfred Owen) or about
   (ii) bees: 'They might ignore me immediately
          In my moonsuit and funeral veil.'   (Sylvia Plath)

4   Repetition

The most obvious repetitions are choruses and chants. They are everyone-join-ins. They join us together in football crowds, skipping, community singing, carol services, gospel sessions. They are crucial parts of work-songs, where working people need to keep time together, as they heave on a rope, or take turns to bash something into the ground. Patriotic songs and soldiers' songs all have things called 'rousing choruses'. They seem to have a uniting, 'aren't-we-glad-we're-us' spirit, (eg *Rule Britannia*) which can turn into the spirit of 'hooray-we're-best' (eg 'Britons never never never shall be slaves') and even into 'boo-to-others' (eg forgetting a history of having enslaved thousands, if not millions, of people in America and the West Indies).

A lot of repetition in poetry has this rousing, stirring, uniting use. The reader or listener or joiner-in has to decide whether to go with or against that powerful urge to join in.

5 Metaphor and simile

Slow
As a limping cow
Or a mighty bull
With its legs split in two
A great black spider comes out of the earth
And climbs up the wall.
Then painfully sets his back against the trees
Throws out his threads for the wind to carry,
Weaves a web that reaches the sky
And spreads his nets across the blue.

JEAN-JOSEPH RABEARIVELO

The poet says the spider is like 'a limping cow/Or a mighty bull/With its legs split in two'. If a writer or a speaker says one thing is 'like' another, this is a *simile*. You will know many ancient or well-used *similes*: as dead as a doornail, as bold as a lion, as cool as a cucumber, as daft as a brush, etc.

The poet says the spider 'spreads his nets'. A spider does not really spread nets, but the poet has, for the moment, turned him into a fisherman, who does. One thing is said to *be* another thing. This is a *metaphor*. 'Spreading nets' is a metaphor for a spider making its web.

Poets use metaphors and similes to do various things.
  (i) It helps them show us how something looks to them.
  (ii) It helps them express an opinion.
 (iii) It helps them alert us to new meanings of old familiar things, to new ideas and feelings.

6 Juxtaposition of images

'Juxtaposition' means the putting of one thing alongside another. Poets juxtapose images. They put the picture (or the idea) of one thing alongside another in ways that you might not expect. They do that as part of the job of alerting our attention to the meaning of what they are trying to say. Juxtaposing of images is yet another way poets try and make their writing *not* ordinary, *not* commonplace, *not* dull.

Sometimes poets don't like to use phrases like 'looked like', 'seems like', 'it felt as if it was', and prefer to give us the image of one thing put alongside another without putting the 'feel as if' in between. That is they juxtapose images in order to communicate feelings immediately. Adrian Mitchell has done that in 'A child is singing'. He wrote it after he heard his four year old niece singing, during a car journey, about 'the total destruction of the world'.

A CHILD IS SINGING

A child is singing
And nobody listening
But the child who is singing:

Bulldozers grab the earth and shower it.
The house is on fire.
Gardeners wet the earth and flower it.
The house is on fire,
The houses are on fire.
Fetch the fire engine, the fire engine's on fire.
We will have to hide in a hole.
We will burn slow like coal.
All the people are on fire.

And a child is singing
And nobody listening
But the child who is singing.

ADRIAN MITCHELL

If ever you find a poem hard to understand, or you can't follow why a particular word or image is used straight after another, or why a phrase brings together two ideas that don't seem to have much to do with each other, then try and see if you can understand it better by putting in 'seemed as if it was . . .' or 'looked as if . . .' or 'it felt like . . .' or 'as though it was a . . .' or 'I felt like . . .' or 'he seemed . . .'. Poets like to leave out phrases and talk to us more directly.

Don't be afraid to say if it doesn't work for you. It means the poet hasn't communicated an idea to you. That could be the poet's fault, or it could be because the poet's culture and your culture are different. The poet conjures up images and pictures from his or her life that you can't see because you have led a different life. Juxtaposing of images is to do with poets' culture – their past, their upbringing, their experiences, all of which supply the poet with his or her image-store. These images might be literally true. ('The house is on fire'.) Or they might be written in what is called 'figurative language', such as metaphors and similes. ('Gardeners . . . flower it', 'We will burn slow like coal'.)

7 Punning

Punning is a way of using words, so that more than one meaning comes over at the same time. Eg what did the policeman say to the tramp asleep under the park bench? You're under a rest.

Here are two poems that use puns:

ALDRIN COLLINS AND ARMSTRONG

```
        5
        4
        3
        2
        1 rocket
        2 the moon
        3 flew it
what 4?
        5
        4
        3
        2
```

MICHAEL ROSEN

Louis he was King of France
before the revolution
Then he had his head chopped off
which spoiled his *constitution*.

TRADITIONAL SEA SHANTY

'Constitution' has two meanings here. 'The French Constitution' means the French system of government. A person's constitution is his or her bodily health. So chopping Louis' head off ruined two things at the same time. But the poem does not *say* that directly – that comes about through the double meaning of the word 'constitution'. Does this make the poem funny? Or to put it another way, when you read the poem do you think you were meant to feel sorry for Louis? Or do you think the poem is in favour of the revolution?

Personally, I think the poem is very clever. It is one verse of many that the man who used to sing to seamen hauling on anchor chains and sailropes, had in his song repertoire nearly two hundred years ago. It's a shanty-man's song. Some English sailors must have thought the French King Louis' head being chopped off was worth a laugh. By expressing it in this clever way – through a pun – it is as if we are asked to laugh at the pun and laugh at the facts of the poem at the same time. A political event or a political character is mocked with wit. This is called *satire*.

Now look at the other poem. I wrote this. It's meant to be a never-ending poem. Countdown, count up, countdown, count up. That, I hope, makes it fun. The countdown is nothing more than a countdown but the count-up has two puns in it, to try and make you laugh and so help me to mock the 'great space-trip'. There *was* one rocket that went to the moon. Three people flew it. What for? (Personally I think it was a waste of time and money.) 'What for?' asks the question which many people don't ask; many people just think going to the moon was 'terrific'. I've tried to mock it, in a way that makes it fun to say, learn and remember.

8   Voices and tone of voice

One of the best examples of this is in the chapter on the War Poems. See *Naming of Parts* on page 85. There the poet imitates the voice of the officer-in-charge of rifle training, without ever saying that's what he is doing. Poets quite often do that: take on a voice or change voice without telling us directly that that is what they're doing.

In *Naming of Parts* there are three voices: the officer-in-charge talking; the poet looking at the gardens and flowers; the phrases where the poet, while remembering the gardens and flowers, hears the voice of the officer-in-charge. The echo-voice. This pushes its way through the day-dreaming voice that is thinking of the gardens and flowers. One voice penetrates another. By using voices he expresses the feeling of day-dreaming – how we do one thing, day-dream about another, and then the sound of the first thing pushes into our day-dream. It is a juxtaposition of voices which in turn produces a very sharp, almost angry juxtaposition of images: rifle-training images set against gardens and flowers.

9   Atmosphere and mood

Poets are people who can use words to conjure up the picture, the sensation of a *place*. They can create *moods* of fear, happiness, regret, joy, anger, loneliness as they conjure up those pictures. These moods are sometimes called 'atmosphere'. In my discussion of *Night Patrol* (page 88), I discuss how the use of the images, the *kind* of images he uses, creates the atmosphere of aloneness.

10   Pattern

This is sometimes called the 'shaping of a poem'. It is done by rhythm or rhyme, or alliteration or repetition, or regular juxtaposition of images or the use of a voice that has an expected way of speaking. A 'blues' is a pattern. A sonnet is a pattern. A ballad (see *Lady Diamond* on page 42) is a pattern. A shanty (see *We Must Choose* on page 36) is a pattern.

Why do poets make their ideas into such patterns? I think the answer to this question depends on whose point of view you want to take – the poet's or the reader's or both! From the poet's point of view, if you can succeed in getting some ideas about life down onto paper in an organised shape, or form, then you have, in a way, made sense out of a problem. You've made sense, an *order*, out of a mass of sensation, feelings, problems, questions, fears, jokes, and created something that can communicate an opinion, a feeling or a purpose to someone else.

From the reader's point of view, following a pattern is part of the process of trying to understand things in the world. If you watch a very young child playing you'll see it doing one thing over and over again – like putting a ball into a saucepan and taking it out again. The baby tries to find a pattern, an order, a predictable shape or rhythm to events. If we can follow the pattern of a poem we might understand the meaning the poet has made out of one particular piece of experience.

In actual fact, following patterns is something we do almost without thinking, joining in choruses, noticing rhymes, following repetitions, following a sequence of images. One measure of powerful, moving, attractive poetry is whether these patterns are used to awaken us, stir us, surprise us.

11 *Emphasis and surprise, breaking the pattern*

This can be done by rhythm, rhyme, repetition, break in flow, juxtaposition of images. It can be done to shock us, to hammer home a point, to make us laugh, to mock, to criticize.

Notice that the blues form in its ideal shape has a natural emphasis in its third line. First line sets up the picture, second line repeats the picture, third line replies, explains, answers, the previous two.

eg I woke up this morning; baby, I had the blues
    I woke up this morning; baby, I had the blues.
    You see me worried, baby, 'cos it's you I hate to lose.

The function of the *second line* is to make sure we have a clear picture, a clear memory, a full sensation of the image or the idea, so that the *third* can come as an emphasized explanation, rebuke, reply, clarification, or contradiction.

People who write poems like to surprise us. It is one of the ways they make us more attentive; make us prick up our ears and listen more carefully. The surprise can come because of a change of rhythm, change of mood, change of voice, a sudden event, a new image, a change in the kind of words used.

eg Humpty Dumpty sat on a wall
    Humpty Dumpty had a great fall
    All the King's horses
    And all the King's men
    Trod on him.
           CHILDREN'S RHYME

ACTIVITY

1 Make a collection of six poems that you know, or that you can find in anthologies, that have different rhythms.
2 Compile a group (or class) list of tongue-twisters.
3 Choose one of the poetic techniques described in this chapter, and use it in a poem about something that interests you. Make sure that the technique is suitable for the attitudes that you want to communicate.
4 Write a blues about one of these subjects: getting up to go to school, the long summer holidays, something you've lost.

I SEE A VOICE

Poetry and society

Inside your head before you say anything or write anything, is a kind of sieve or strainer. This strainer lets 'somethings' through and holds other things back. These 'somethings' are the words, sayings and sentences of what you are going to say. You, as a speaker or writer, *choose* from thousands of words and sayings in your head exactly the ones you want. Of course, it doesn't always work that smoothly:

I have forgotten the word
I intended to say
And my thought
Unembodied
Returns to the realm of shadows.
O MANDELSTAM

Everything you say or write is *said* or *written* because you have some idea who you're saying it for or who you're saying it to. In plain talk – you talk one way to one person and a different way to someone else. That's you 'knowing your audience'.

Who taught you to know your audience?

It's you that do it but it's you having been many times (i) a watcher of *others* (ii) a receiver, a listener to *others* (iii) a speaker to *others*.

So now let's look at something you have said. Remember when you were small? When some of you picked up sides for a game or chose someone to be 'it' or 'on' or 'on it', you said:

Eena meena
macka racka
rare ra
dominnacker
chickerbocker
lollypopper
om
pom
PUSH

or something like it.

It's a rhyme.
Let's look back to see how you learned it.
(i)   When you were young, you saw older boys and girls using this rhyme (or others like it) to play their games.
(ii)   When you were a bit older you actually joined in the circle when someone said the rhyme and you obeyed the rules of the rhyme: whoever the PUSH ended up on had to be 'it' or 'on'.
(iii)   Then you learnt it, chose to use it because (i) and (ii) seemed to have worked out OK – and hey presto – when you used it, it worked out fine for you. You, the poet in *your* social group, your mini-society.

BUT what happened if you moved away from where people say 'eena meena macka racka' to a place where people say 'Ippi dippi dation, My operation'? Then they may have thought you were a twit going through all that 'eena meena' rubbish. Or they may have thought you were pretty clever to have learnt off this tricky little rhyme.

So that was you, the poet, in a *different* situation. Did they change you and stop using 'eena meena' or did you change them and get them to use yours?

When you're trying to understand a poem better, it's often helpful to think of the situation it was written for. What was the audience the poet had in mind? And what was the writer's purpose?

28

ACTIVITY

1. *Eight poems/songs*

   Choose a group of eight poems and songs you know and write down their words. Make them as varied as possible.

   eg A playground rhyme you remember
   A song someone sings in your home
   A funny rhyme you know
   A song you were taught at school
   A dialect poem
   A football chant or song

2. *When I learned*

Title of poem/song	Who taught me	Where	When	Social Group present

   When you've made your list in (1), write down

   who you learnt each one of them off (if you can remember)

   where you learnt it

   what *kind of occasion* was it? eg a party, playing in the playground

   were you on your own? or in a group?

3. *My performances*

   Look again at each item on your list of poems and songs. Can you remember the last time you sang or said it?
   Where was it? What kind of occasion was it? Why did you sing/say it?

4. When you have done (a), (b) and (c), you have in front of you a kind of map of yourself in your world. It is a picture (in words) of (i) the company you have kept in the past, (ii) some of the poems and songs you have picked up, (iii) you as a performer.

   Now compare *your* map with other people around you. Find out what you have in common with them and what's different.

SONG OF AGONY

I put on a clean shirt
and go to work my contract
   Which of us
   Which of us will come back?
Four and twenty moons
not seeing women
not seeing my ox
not seeing my land
   Which of us
   Which of us will die?
I put on a clean shirt
and go to work my contract
to work far away
I go beyond the mountain
into the bush
where the road ends
and the river runs dry.
   Which of us
   Which of us will come back?
   Which of us
   Which of us will die?

GOUVEIA DE LEMOS

The song of a contract worker – that is to say, a person who works for someone for a short amount of time like a month or a summer season. Here are some contract workers: Mexicans who travel into the Southern States of the USA to pick fruit; Portuguese and Spanish people who come to work in the hotels, cafés and restaurants in London; Black Africans from the townships, bantustans and countries surrounding South Africa, who travel into South Africa to work in the mines; building workers (often from Western Ireland) who travel to England to work as navvies, bricklayers, scaffoldmen on the building sites and motorway construction; Turks who travel to Germany and so on and so on.

It is the viewpoint of one person, but it represents a viewpoint of a whole group of people – migrant contract workers. This group has a relationship with the country (or the society) that employs the people of the group. Quite often they are despised, even hated, laughed at, harrassed. Quite often these migrant workers and their children are described as having 'no culture'. Out of this background Gouveia de Lemos speaks. It is the viewpoint of the person who 'society' often thinks of as the outsider, but who 'society' needs and benefits from. With this poem we are in a sense privileged to hear the viewpoint of a group in society who we normally only hear about because other people complain about them.

Here is a poet then who is not expressing, say, the culture of the Royal Family; the culture of the Youth; the culture of mums and dads on holiday, the culture of women, but the culture of the outsider, and the despised. The poet's purpose then could have been two-fold: firstly, to represent the contract-worker's condition so that other people in a similar situation could see themselves in his description; secondly, to reach the ears of people in society who (i) might be unaware of these workers' condition, who (ii) might not care about these conditions or who (iii) might even be the people who have created these conditions.

One way of looking at poems is to try and sort out where the poet stands in society. That is to say, what are the poet's opinions about events in his or her country or the world? Do the poet's works show these opinions?

One of the reasons why we might look at the poet in his or her society is because everyone's ideas come out of their experience of the society they live in. You can try this out yourselves. Take for example ideas about 'beauty'. You probably have ideas about someone who is beautiful, a place that is beautiful, a building that is beautiful, maybe even a beautiful thing to say.

Now you could find other people in your group that disagree with you. You could read about people from different countries that disagree. You could find people older than you, of a different sex to you, from a different part of the country to you, from a different class in society to you – and you'd all disagree about what is beautiful. Why?

I think it all depends on people's experience of the place they live and what the people they meet and live with think: If you were a gangster or a soldier you'd think some guns were beautiful. If you were a gardener you might think a tulip was beautiful but a daisy in the middle of your lawn was ugly. Many of these opinions about beauty and ugliness come about because important voices reach our ears informing us, commanding us and influencing us. Eg teachers, parents, politicians, the Church, and advertising.

WRANGLER JEANS

Five pairs of Wrangler Jeans
Bursting out the door
One pair left his bike in bits
Then there were four

Four pairs of Wrangler Jeans
With a flat old battery
One pair pushed a bit too hard
Then there were three

Three pairs of Wrangler Jeans
Standing in a queue
One pair knew the Manager
Then there were two

Two pairs of Wrangler Jeans
About to have some fun
Big brother says, Out of order'
Then there was one

Now the moral of this story
Is: if they desert you in the end,
As long as you wear Wrangler
You've got a real two-legged friend.

JOHN KELLEY/JOHN O'DRISCOLL

Are Wrangler Jeans beautiful? This year maybe, next year maybe not. Why? Because our society depends on a fast turnover of clothes, records, cars, record-players, stereos and hundreds of other goods that are enjoyable luxuries that may wear out very quickly. Our society depends on people like me and you changing our mind on what is beautiful from year to year so that we'll keep spending our money to buy something new. You can argue whether this is a good or bad thing in itself but consider the two ideas – making something so it'll *sell* immediately as opposed to making something so it'll be useful.

This is why the Wrangler Jeans poem has been written. It is not in order to point out the usefulness of Wrangler Jeans but simply in order to convince you that they must be bought *now*. Advertising 'art' does not require you to buy the poem or the poster; it requires you to walk into a shop and buy the thing the poem or poster talks about. We've now reached a time in our society where many of the poems and songs we hear every day try to make us buy something.

This means that our feelings and opinions about many things (eg beauty, food, ways of spending our time, hair-style, the way we talk to each other, the things that women ought to do) are linked with what the ads tell us. Behind the scenes there is a battle: Wrangler Jeans vs Levi Jeans vs Lois Jeans vs Lee Jeans. Someone has to win, someone has to lose. Ads' poetry is about trying to make you back one to win. Of course you may not have enough money to back the winner. Then every night you listen to advertising art that will tell you that you are inadequate unless you do what they say: Buy me, buy me, buy me.

We are told that the wealth of this country depends on this outpouring of art and poetry – because that makes the system work. I wonder how much we gain by this and how much we lose.

ACTIVITY

1. Would you write poetry to get people to buy things? If you can't afford to look like the people in the ads, does that make you feel rotten? Write your feelings about these questions as a poem or an essay, or include them in a story.

2. Let's consider the whole society in which you learnt your poems and songs. Write down the titles of *five* poems or songs that you think most people in Britain would know. What are they about? Where and when are they performed? To whom? Why? Who organizes those performances? Who, apart from young children, would probably not know them?

Title	Subject-matter	Performance	Audience	Purpose	Organizer
You'll never walk alone	There is a power that will support you through difficulties.	Football terraces	Crowds at football matches	Ritual way to express a spirit of solidarity	Fans

Frankie Armstrong singing at a Trico demonstration

Here is a voice

'Many of the songs I sing are of relevance to "today", to "everybody today".'

Frankie Armstrong

Frankie Armstrong is a singer. She sings songs that she herself has written; songs written by people she knows; songs written by people she doesn't know; and songs made up by no-one knows who. Many of them express views on subjects that she feels strongly about.

The collection of songs is called her *repertoire*. It is a collection of songs chosen from thousands she has heard, thousands she likes, hundreds she knows.

1   *We must choose*

In this country there are a lot of people who are strongly opposed to abortion. They believe that to have an abortion is, unnecessarily, to take human life. In a society where some men and women believe such things, Frankie Armstrong wrote a song putting the views of many people who think differently about abortion – that it should be a woman's right to choose whether to have an abortion or not. Her song was written for an occasion: a rally and demonstration for the National Abortion Campaign in 1976.

WE MUST CHOOSE

Sisters we are singing
We must choose
Brothers join us singing
We must choose
For ten thousand years
We must choose
We have born our kids in fear
We must choose
And still we're fighting to be free
We must choose
Don't let them turn back history
We must choose
Sisters sing it out in chorus
We must choose
Don't let them do our choosing for us
We must choose
We'll not be shouted down or cheated
We must choose
We'll see this Benyon Bill defeated
We must choose
Enough of fears and sorrow
We must choose
We'll build a better world tomorrow
We must choose
A world where every child born
We must choose
Will be a rose and not a thorn
We must choose
We must choose, Yes
We must choose
Will we win or will we lose?
WE MUST CHOOSE.

FRANKIE ARMSTRONG

'She stood at the microphone, she taught her audience how to sing the chorus and then she started to sing her lines. Soon the whole of Trafalgar Square was singing with her and listening to her. As an occasion, it helped draw us together; it helped us campaign for what we believed in, it was a way of saying, a way of doing, a way of living, a way of enjoying, a way of fighting for an idea.'

Anyone who has been in a football crowd, a gospel-singing church, concert or street carnival has probably experienced the same or similar thing.

'What was especially exciting was that Frankie was singing something she had made up for that moment then. At that moment no-one knew *what* was coming next, what *idea* would come next, what new twist she had in store. All that you knew was that there was another line coming. The pattern of the song told us that, didn't it?'

She was a poet in her 'society'.

2   *I'm gonna be an engineer*

Frankie knows many song-writers. One – Peggy Seeger – has written songs that are critical of much in our society.

For instance, if you are a young woman then there are certain things expected of you by your mother, teachers, grandma, neighbours, friends, boyfriend, father – especially when it comes to love, marriage, babies, jobs.

One of Peggy's songs, sung by Frankie Armstrong, is called *I'm gonna be an engineer*. This doesn't mean that either Peggy or Frankie necessarily want to be engineers. It's more like 'what-if-I-did wanna be an engineer'. But it tells a story too.

I'm gonna be an engineer was first sung in a room above a pub in North London. Now it's known and sung all over the world by women who want to say something about men-and-women in society. It is a perfect example of how a song can be popular without having to be a 'pop' song, how a poem can be known all over the world without appearing in 'A Book of Poetry'. I think this is because what people *buy*, what people *say* they want, and what people might *really* want, are all very different things. And inside every person are disagreements and arguments going on. Songs and poems like *I'm gonna be an engineer* pick quarrels with people. They can make us think about society.

I'M GONNA BE AN ENGINEER

Easily

When I was a lit-tle girl I wished I was a boy,   I
tagged a-long be-hind the gang and wore my cor-dur-oys,
Eve-ry-bod-y said I on-ly did it to an-noy, But I was
gon-na be an en - gi - neer.
Mom-ma told me 'Can't you be a la - dy? Your
du-ty is to make me the moth-er of a pearl.
Wait un-til you're old-er, dear, and may - be
You'll be glad that you're a girl.'

(this part only after verses 1,3,6 and 7)

Dain-ty as a dres-den sta-tue,
Gen-tle as a jer-sey cow; Smooth as silk, Gives

38

cream- y milk: Learn to coo, Learn to moo,

That's what it takes to be a lad - y now.

When I went to school I learned to write and how to read,
Some history, geography and home economy,
And typing is a skill that every girl is sure to need
To while away the extra time until the time to breed.
And then they had to nerve to say, 'What would you like to be?'
I says 'I'm gonna be an engineer!'

No, you only need to learn to be a lady,
The duty isn't yours, for to try and run the world,
An engineer could never have a baby,
Remember, dear, that you're a girl.

So I become a typist and I study on the sly,
Working out the day and night so I can qualify,
And every time the boss come in he pinched me on the thigh,
Says, 'I've never had an engineer!'

You owe it to the job to be a lady,
It's the duty of the staff for to give the boss a whirl,
The wages that you get are crummy, maybe,
But it's all you get cos you're a girl.

She's smart (for a woman)
I wonder how she got that way?
You get no choice,
You get no voice,
Just stay mum,
Pretend you're dumb,
That's how you come to be a lady today.

Then Jimmy come along and we set up a conjugation,
We were busy every night with loving recreation,
I spent my days at work so he could get his education
And now he's an engineer!

He says, 'I know you'll always be a lady
It's the duty of my darling to love me all her life.
Could an engineer look after or obey me?
Remember, dear, that you're my wife!'

As soon as Jimmy got a job I studied hard again,
Then, busy at me turret-lathe a year or so, and then
The morning that the twins were born, Jimmy says to them,
'Kids, your mother was an engineer.'

You owe it to the kids to be a lady,
Dainty as a dish-rag, faithful as a chow,
Stay at home, you've got to mind the baby
Remember you're a mother now.

Every time I turn around there's something else to do,
Cook a meal or mend a sock or sweep a floor or two,
I listen in to Jimmy Young, it makes me want to spew,
I was gonna be an engineer.

I really wish that I could be a lady,
I could do the lovely things that a lady's s'posed to do,
I wouldn't mind if only they would pay me.
And I could be a person too.

> *What price—for a woman?*
> *You can buy her for a ring of gold;*
> *To love and obey*
> *(Without any pay)*
> *You get a cook or a nurse,*
> *For better or worse,*
> *You don't need a purse when a lady is sold.*

But now that times are harder, and my Jimmy's got the sack,'
I went down to Vickers, they were glad to have me back,
I'm a third-class citizen, my wages tell me that,
But I'm a first-class engineer,

The boss he says, 'I pay you as a lady,
You only got the job cos I can't afford a man.
With you I keep the profits high as may be,
You're just a cheaper pair of hands.'

You've got one fault: you're a woman,
You're not worth; the equal pay,
A bitch or a tart,
You're nothing but heart,
Shallow and vain,
You got no brain,
Go down the drain like a lady today.

I listened to my mother and I joined a typing pool,
I listened to my lover and I sent him through his school,
If I listen to the boss, I'm just a bloody fool,
And an underpaid engineer.

I've been a sucker ever since I was a baby,
As a daughter, as a wife, as a mother and a dear,
But I'll fight them as a woman, not a lady,
I'll fight them as an engineer.

PEGGY SEEGER

ACTIVITY

1. Read, or listen to, one of the songs. Then write down or discuss your reactions to the questions:

    (i) Did it change your mind about anything?
    (ii) If it changes *your* mind, who else's mind could it change? Could it change thousands of minds?
    (iii) Who might see it as a 'dangerous' song?

2. Write a poem or song that would make your friends (or enemies) think hard about something. Try any of these: marriage, fashion, prejudice, people who think they are superior, the homeless, closing down of factories or hospitals, money, laws, a newspaper or TV programme.

3. Your poem or song from (2) is a sign of where you stand in society. Read it in a group with others. *Listen* to what people say when they've heard what you've written. Then you can listen to what they've written.

4. Choose a topic in a group. Work out where you agree/disagree. Write a poem setting out some things you all agree about; a poem that starts 'We believe . . .' or 'We don't want . . .' or 'We care about . . .' or 'We will . . .'

Frankie Armstrong and others go about the country singing this story to various audiences – young people, old people, young people in care, family groups, in clubs, etc.

LADY DIAMOND

There was a king, and a glorious king,
  A king of noble fame,
And he had daughters only one,
  Lady Diamond was her name.

He had a boy, a kitchen boy,
  A boy of muckle scorn,*   *who was despised
She loved him long, she loved him aye,
  Till the grass o'er grew the corn.

When twenty weeks were gone and past,
  O she began to greet,†   †weep
For her petticoats grew short before,
  And her stays they wouldn't meet.

It fell upon one winter's night,
  The king could get no rest,
He came unto his daughter dear,
  Just like a wandering ghost.

He came unto her bed chamber,
  Pulled back the curtains long,
'What aileth thee my daughter dear,
  I fear you have gotten wrong.'

'O if I have, despise me not,
  For he is all my joy,
I will forsake both dukes and earls
  And marry your kitchen boy.'

'O bring to me my merry men all,
    By thirty and by three,
O bring to me my kitchen boy,
    We'll murder him secretly.'

There was not a sound into the hall,
    And ne'er a word was said,
Until they got him safe and sure,
    Between two feather beds.

'Cut the heart from out of his breast,
    Put it in a cup of gold,
And present it to his Diamond dear,
    For she was both stout and bold.'

'O come to me, my hinnie, my heart,‡   ‡my dear
    O come to me my joy,
O come to me my hinnie, my heart,
    My father's kitchen boy.'

She took the cup from out of their hands,
    And she set it at her bed head.
She washed it with tears that fell from her eyes,
    And next morning she was dead.

'O where were you my merry men all,
    That I gave meat and wage,
That you didn't stay my cruel hand,
    When I was in a rage?

For gone is all my heart's delight,
    O gone is all my joy,
For my dear Diamond she is dead,
    Likewise my kitchen boy.'

TRADITIONAL BALLAD

Lady Diamond was written by no-one-knows-who. It has been sung by thousands of people all over the world for hundreds for years. They didn't sell it; they didn't go into a frenzy over the singer. They sang it, talked about it, carried it about in their heads, forgot bits of it, added bits to it, dreamt about it, acted out bits of it, and maybe tried not to be as wicked as the most wicked people in the story. And while these thousands of people over the years were singing and changing the story, wars were fought, villages burnt down. Kings and Queens lived and died, towns grew up, ships came and went, fevers, plagues and fires passed through. And people still went on thinking it was a story-poem worth singing.

The song probably started out its life 500 or 600 years ago, when the events of the story could have been actual happenings in the households of the high and mighty. It is, then, a song made for a different society, but one where the rights and wrongs of the things people do to each other can still make us sad or angry or have some other feeling.

ACTIVITY

1.   (i) Do you think the king is sorry for what he did?
   (ii) Do you think his 'merry men' could have said, 'No, we won't kill your kitchen boy'?
  (iii) Why do you think a king's daughter would want to go off with a kitchen boy?
  (iv) Why would that make a king so angry?
   (v) Does the story make you cross?, sad?, indignant?
  (vi) Do you 'take sides' like you do when you hear two people having a row? Whose side are you on?
 (vii) Compare your answers to these questions with a partner's answers. Give reasons for any differences of opinion.

2.   (i) Rewrite the story of the poem from the point of view of one of the characters, including feelings about what happens.
  (ii) Write a conversation beween *either* the king and his men *or* Lady Diamond and the kitchen boy.

3.   Write a review of *Lady Diamond* or one of the other songs in this chapter, saying briefly what the song is about, and what your feelings are about that.

QUESTIONS OF LOVE

A girl once showed me a poem she had written. In it she said how the boy she liked so much didn't seem to know that she was so keen on him. So I said to her:
'Well why don't you tell him?'
'I couldn't do that.'
'Why not?'
'The shame of it', she said, 'I couldn't do that!'
So I said, 'Could you send him this poem?'
'Oh no – that'd be even worse. I'd be giving everything away'.

What do you make of that? She had written down her true feelings. She had written down that it was terrible he didn't know her true feelings; but then she told me it would be even worse if he *did* know her true feelings because she'd be giving too much away. Does that sound right to you? It didn't to me.

I like to think of poems sometimes as a bit like seeds that need fertile ground to grow in. Poems need a fertile ground. What is the fertile ground for *love* poetry? Quite often it's when you can't say out loud how you feel, like that girl. Here is a list of such occasions:
— when you are away from each other
— when you want to say something very simple but very important so you want it to last a long time
— when you don't want to say it out loud because you're afraid you'll say it wrong
— when you don't know why you feel the way you do
— when you feel ashamed and don't want to hear yourself being told off
— when you're afraid of giving away too much
— when you think you might be laughed at for saying something soppy.

45

All those situations (and there must be millions of others) are like spaces where love poems like to grow up. It's *their* fertile ground. They are the gaps left because
— the time wasn't right
— the place wasn't right
— or it didn't feel right
to say it out loud.

FIRST LOVE

I ne'er was struck before that hour
   With love so sudden and so sweet.
   Her face it bloomed like a sweet flower
   And stole my heart away complete.
My face turned pale as deadly pale,
   My legs refused to walk away,
And when she looked 'what could I ail?'
   My life and all seemed turned to clay.

And then my blood rushed to my face
   And took my sight away.
The trees and bushes round the place
   Seemed midnight at noonday.
I could not see a single thing,
   Words from my eyes did start;
They spoke as chords do from the string,
   And blood burnt round my heart.

Are flowers the winter's choice?
   Is love's bed always snow?
She seemed to hear my silent voice
   And love's appeal to know.

I never saw so sweet a face
   As that I stood before:
My heart has left its dwelling-place
   And can return no more.

JOHN CLARE

So love poetry is born out of 'situations' that somebody wants to write down some feelings about. When I read love poetry I try to find my way back to those 'situations', so that I can enjoy and understand the poem. I have to recognise it – maybe as something I have been through myself; maybe as something I have seen others going through; something I remember; or something I wished had happened to me. In other words, the love poem gives something to me and I bring something to it.

MANWATCHING

From across the party I watch you,
Watching her.
Do my possessive eyes
Imagine your silent messages?
I think not.
She looks across at you
And telegraphs her flirtatious reply.
I have come to recognize this code,
You are on intimate terms with this pretty stranger,
And there is nothing I can do,
My face is calm, expressionless,
But my eyes burn into your back.
While my insides shout with rage.
She weaves her way towards you,
Turning on a bewitching smile.
I can't see your face, but you are mesmerised I expect.
I can predict you: I know this scene so well,
Some acquaintance grabs your arm,
You turn and meet my accusing stare head on,
Her eyes follow yours, meet mine,
And then slide away, she understands,
She's not interested enough to compete.
It's over now.
She fades away, you drift towards me,
'I'm bored' you say, without a trace of guilt,
So we go.
Passing the girl in the hall.
'Bye' I say frostily,
I suppose
You winked.

GEORGIA GARRETT

FIRST ICE

A girl freezes in a telephone booth.
In her draughty overcoat she hides
A face all smeared
In tears and lipstick.

She breathes on her thin palms.
Her fingers are icy. She wears earrings.

She'll have to go home alone, alone,
Along the icy street.

First ice. It is the first time.
The first ice of telephone phrases.

Frozen tears glitter on her cheeks –
The first ice of human hurt.

ANDREY VOZNESENSKY

ACTIVITY

Choose one of the above love poems and then see whether you can do this:
1. Write about 'the fertile ground' the poem has grown up in. What is the gap or space it fills?
2. Write about the feelings and situations talked about in the poem.
3. What feelings, memories or hopes does the poem *remind* you of?

A *single* incident or picture is called 'particular' or 'specific', but when people describe something so that it can refer to a lot of specific things at the same time – that is 'abstract' or 'general'. Words like 'love' or 'anger' are abstract – general words that poets (amongst other people) often try to help us understand by giving 'specific' examples of what they mean.

In *Love is . . .*, Adrian Henri keeps saying what 'love is' for him and his lover. It's a way of explaining a very difficult word in a very simple way. He isn't defining what it means for other people. It's not the kind of description you'd find in a dictionary. It's his own personal Adrian Henri dictionary.

48

LOVE IS . . .

Love is feeling cold in the back of vans
Love is a fanclub with only two fans
Love is walking holding paintstained hands
Love is

Love is fish and chips on winter nights
Love is blankets full of strange delights
Love is when you don't put out the light
Love is

Love is the presents in Christmas shops
Love is when you're feeling Top of the Pops
Love is what happens when the music stops
Love is

Love is white panties lying all forlorn
Love is a pink nightdress still slightly warm
Love is when you have to leave at dawn
Love is

Love is you and love is me
Love is a prison and love is free
Love's what's there when you're away from me
Love is . . .

ADRIAN HENRI

One of the ways we can learn about life is by writing down what a certain moment or feeling means to us – and then sharing that writing with other people. Here it's a bit like a public letter. Adrian Henri talks straight to his lover calling her 'you' as if she's there listening. He has made her his first audience. After that we come in as his second audience.

Each 'love is' is a little picture – a small incident in their lives, apart from the last three.

'Love is you and love is me
 Love is a prison and love is free
 Love's what's there when you're away from me.'

Adrian Henri changes the rhythm and at the same time changes the kind of 'love' he is talking about.

In these last lines, Adrian Henri is trying to sum up his lists of specific meanings of love into a total meaning.
'Love is you'. That is to say 'it's *all* of you'.
'love is me'. That is 'it's *all* of me'.
But because these two phrases are so close together in rhythm, I think Adrian Henri is saying: Love is all of you and all of me, *together*.

Then, 'Love is a prison and love is free'.
These two phrases may seem to be a contradiction. You might say, 'How can love be a prison and at the same time be free?' This is a difference between poetry and science. If you want to describe something in science or maths, you can't make that 'something' mean two things that are completely opposite to each other. You can't write, 'Oxygen in air is a gas and oxygen in air is a solid'. But in poetry you can write opposites in order to point out a *paradox**.

'Love is a prison and love is free.' Why? I won't try to answer that question, but you might see whether you can think of reasons why both these statements can be true.

Now look at the last statement:
'Love's what's there when you're away from me'.
That's a paradox as well. Earlier in the poem he said 'love is you' but here he says that love is when 'you' are not there. Love is what he's left with when his lover has gone. That, of course, is a feeling. All the pictures in the other parts of the poem were happenings and events. This final statement is the feeling he has *after* all those happenings.

*A paradox is when something seems contradictory; for instance, it may seem absurd and sensible at the same time. Here is a paradox about water:
Water gives life (to plants) and takes life (from a drowning man).
And here's another paradox:
Mortar keeps bricks in a wall together; mortar keeps bricks in a wall apart.

ACTIVITY

Take a word like Love or Anger or Hunger or Fun or Sadness, and then write down some of the different things that that word means to you – or all the different *times* the word has meant something to you.

eg

Hunger is going to the fridge
and finding nothing in it.
Hunger is walking past Macdonalds
with no money in your pocket.

or

Anger is when my sister
tells me to find her slippers.
Anger is when I miss the bus.

SHE SAID

She said:—You were very nice, quiet and polite,
She said:—You were considerate, well brought up,
She said:—You were happy and kind,
She knows you live 200 miles away,
She just can't understand us.

She knows I don't see enough of you,
She certainly makes sure of that,
She said I think of you too much,
She just can't understand us.

She said phone calls were too frequent,
She said they must stop; then relented and
She said two calls a week was enough,
She said ten minutes is sufficient for any news you've got.
She listens in I know she does,
She just can't understand us.

She saw my exam results,
She said that was the limit,
She asked what was in your letters that made me so distant,
She reads them now – then gives them to me.
She said that was the only way to prevent it.
I said 'Prevent what?'
She said she didn't understand me.

She said my letters were to be approved at first,
She said she'd read then post them,
She said she would,
She said any arguments were in vain,
She said I was too young,
She said you'd get tired then what would I do – no qualifications no job,
She doesn't understand us.

She said she'd posted my letters,
She said you haven't written back,
You are getting them aren't you,
She said you would she said
She said – she lied.

She's hurting me,
She's hurting you and your family,
She said – she says – she has said,
She will say – she will say no longer!
She cried when I left!
I don't understand her.

LIZ HUTCHINS

This is another poem that proceeds by showing us one view after another of the same thing. The thing in this case is 'she', Liz Hutchins' mother.

Character

In talking about stories, films, plays or poems, people often use the word 'character'. It means two things – (i) a person (ii) the personality of a person. So in Liz Hutchins' poem, as in many poems, we can ask ourselves: what is the 'character' of the person in this poem? And how is the character created? The main person here is mother. Quite often people describe a person's character by (i) what they look like (ii) what the writer thinks is going on in that person's mind (iii) what the person does. But in this poem we learn about Liz's mother mostly, but not entirely, from what Liz tells us her mother *says*.

Plot

Secondly, we can talk about 'plot'. Like 'character' this is a word that people use when they look closely at films, stories, plays and, sometimes, poems. Basically it means 'story' or the brief outline (or summary) of the story. You could say the 'plot' of the gospels in the New Testament of the Bible is: A man who is acclaimed as the son of God was born in a stable, performed many miracles and was killed on a cross by the Romans.

The 'plot' of *this* poem is revealed in the same way as the character. That is, by telling us what Liz Hutchins' mother said. So 'character' and 'plot' are told at the same time and in the same way. Or, to put it another way, character and plot 'develop' together. Liz Hutchins hasn't simply written down all the things she remembers her mother saying, in any old random order. She has chosen which of her mother's words to put first, second, third and so on, so that we are told a story, step by step.

Also the poem seems to tell the story of Liz Hutchins' relationship with her boyfriend almost entirely through the mother's eyes. I say 'almost' because Liz Hutchins does let us know that she doesn't approve of what her mother says and does. For example, she tells us that her mother 'does not understand' them. We are made to feel that what the mother says is more and more outrageous.

Like Adrian Henri's poem, *She said* talks about 'you'. It's another 'public letter' poem. We are listening in on one end of a conversation.* This makes the poem very dramatic, very direct. A stream of emotion is directed straight to her boyfriend, as if she is not bothering to explain anything to us, the readers.

This poem, I believe, is dramatic because it unfolds incidents and a character with a growing feeling of tension. This is not tension of an exciting kind, but more of an ominous, doomed kind. We approach a crisis in the story. If this story is read with a range of tone and mood then the dramatic quality of the poem can be increased. That may seem very obvious but many people forget that our speaking voices can and do express so much by tone alone. It is my opinion that poems like this one only really begin to live and matter to us when they are expressed out loud. The route to understanding and enjoying a dramatic poem like this one is through finding the best way to say it out loud.

*Think of the difference between
(1) overhearing someone saying to someone else 'Of course, I love you';
(2) someone saying to you 'I told him I loved him';
(3) someone telling you 'I heard her say she loved him'.

That's three ways of describing a conversation. I think the overhearing one is the most intimate and seemingly the most truthful. The other two ways are at one and two steps removed from the first incident because they are in 'reported' speech, reporting on an event. Any of these ways of conveying something may be used by a poet. In Liz Hutchins' poem, we are in on some 'overhearing'.

ACTIVITY

1. Try to describe a person's character by just writing down the things that that person says and/or does. Put in some of your opinions as well, if you wish.

2. Read *She said* by Liz Hutchins on page 52. What stages can you see in this poem?

3. Try writing down line by line for the poem, a word to describe what tone of voice Liz Hutchins is using, or what tone of voice you would use in reading it aloud to someone.

   Here are some words you might find useful: mocking, angry, bitter, sad, apologising (apologetic), sneering, resigned (ie when you shrug your shoulders and say 'it can't be helped'), complaining, sorry, ruthless, precise, analytic, contemptuous, whining.

4. Try writing down a conversation you heard, or a conversation that you've taken part in. Then try and turn it into a conversation that someone else heard and was telling to you.

5. Think of an event involving you. Write down the things people said as the event took place, but only write down those things that help the story to develop.

   Then look back at what you've written and see whether the statements you have written down also reveal the personality and character of the people. If not, write a second version so that they do.

6. People often sing or write poems to the one they love saying all the fantastic things they'd do for the one they love – they'd run round the world or swim the seven seas.

   Write a poem or song or just make a list of very real things you could do for your loved one.

7. Write a poem in which you pretend to be someone wondering if they love you. He or she is weighing up your good and bad features.

8. (i) Write a piece called 'The Love Trap' and explain to your readers why they must never fall in love because of the sadness, sorrow, inconvenience or violence it causes.

   (ii) Then write a reply showing why loving is the best thing on earth. You could write it like an argument between two people or between two voices like this:

   Love: I am beautiful and make people warm.
   Anti-love: You eat people up with jealousy.

Again and again songs and poems seem to become *part* of the loves in our lives. The song or the poem seems to say something about a situation better than we could. It's a song or poem that opened our eyes to a new *truth* about loving.

This can be because it shows us a different way of loving; tragic outcomes of a way of loving; or happy outcomes of a way of loving and so on.

It might be a reminding-type poem – reminding you of something in your life. Or a truth-telling type. Telling you of feelings you would like to have, afraid you have, afraid you don't have. Or it may be so strong in its effect because of its sound, its music, that you are simply pulled into a pool of emotion and you like to stay in that pool for a bit.

ACTIVITY

(i)   Write down the titles of three poems or songs which have meant a lot to you.

(ii) Can you describe exactly what moment the poem or song came into your life?

(iii) Can you describe what it does for you?

FIGHTING BACK

BACK IN THE PLAYGROUND BLUES

Dreamed I was in a school playground, I was about four feet high
Yes dreamed I was back in the playground and standing about four feet
high
The playground was three miles long and the playground was five miles
wide

It was broken black tarmac with a high fence all around
Broken black dusty tarmac with a high fence running all around
And it had a special name to it, they called it The Killing Ground.

Got a mother and a father, they're a thousand miles away
The Rulers of the Killing Ground are coming out to play
Everyone thinking: who they going to play with today?

   You get it for being Jewish
   Get it for being black
   Get it for being chicken
   Get it for fighting back
   You get it for being big and fat
   Get it for being small
   O those who get it get it and get it
   For any damn thing at all

Sometimes they take a beetle, tear off its six legs one by one
Beetle on its black back rocking in the lunchtime sun
But a beetle can't beg for mercy, a beetle's not half the fun

Heard a deep voice talking, it had that iceberg sound;
'It prepares them for Life' – but I have never found
Any place in my life that's worse than The Killing Ground.

ADRIAN MITCHELL

Over the years, thousands of poems have been written to express disagreement, opposition, aggro, dislike, hate with certain goings-on in the society the poet lived in. People have written songs and poems that try and expose injustice and change opinion.

One way of trying to make up your mind about what you believe in, in *this* world, is to read what other people wrote about *their* worlds. Poets like Wilfred Owen and Siegfried Sassoon writing about the First World War:

THE GENERAL

'Good morning; good morning!' the General said
When we met him last week on our way to the line.
Now the soldiers he smiled at are most of 'em dead,
And we're cursing his staff for incompetent swine.
'He's a cheery old card,' grunted Harry to Jack
As they slogged up to Arras with rifle and pack

* * * *

But he did for them both by his plan of attack.

SIEGFRIED SASSOON

Songwriters like Tom Paxton, singing in America today:

WHAT DID YOU LEARN IN SCHOOL TODAY?

What did you learn in school today, dear little boy of mine?
What did you learn in school today, dear little boy of mine?

1. I learned that Washington never told a lie;
   I learned that soldiers seldom die;
   I learned that everybody's free,
   And that's what the teacher said to me.
   And that's what I learned in school today
   That's what I learned in school.

2. I learned that policemen are my friends,
   I learned that justice never ends,
   I learned that murderers die for their crimes,
   Even if we make a mistake sometimes.

3. I learned our government must be strong,
   It's always right and never wrong,
   Our leaders are the finest men,
   And we elect 'em again and again.

4. I learned that war is not so bad,
   I learned about the great ones we have had,
   We fought in Germany and in France,
   And someday I might get my chance.

TOM PAXTON

Shelley writing about *his* society in the early nineteenth century:

TO THE MEN OF ENGLAND

Men of England, wherefore plough
For the lords who lay ye low?
Wherefore weave with toil and care
The rich robes your tyrants wear?

Wherefore feed, and clothe, and save,
From the cradle to the grave,
Those ungrateful drones who would
Drain your sweat – nay, drink your blood.

    . . .

So seed, – but let no tyrant reap;
Find wealth, – let no imposter heap;
Weave robes, – let not the idle wear;
Forge arms, – in your defence to bear.

    . . .

P. B. SHELLEY

It's very easy to find poems and songs that agree with, glorify, and celebrate happenings in society. The anthems, the tributes to leaders, the songs of praise, eg *God save the Queen* or *The Charge of the Light Brigade*.

The poems and songs of opposition sometimes only reach their audience because they were nailed to a tree, sold for a penny a time on street corners, read out at meetings, passed secretly between people in army barracks, prisons, workhouses, behind people's backs. Here's one like that:

THE SONG OF THE UPRISING IN PENTRIDGE 1817

Every man his skill must try
He must turn out and not deny
No bloody soldiers must he dread
He must turn out and fight for bread
The time is come you plainly see
When government opposed must be

LUDDITE POEM

Contemporary hostile cartoon of rioting Luddites

ACTIVITY

1. Make a list of five things you'd like to protest about and say why.

2. You can change people's minds in a number of ways: eg make someone sorry for what they've done; make someone afraid to do something again because they know you'll protest about it; get other people to see things your way so they'll join in your protest. Write a poem or song or rhyme or riddle that tries to change somebody's mind. It could begin:
    'I accuse . . .'
    'I'll tell you the story of how they (or we) . . .'
    'Look at the way they . . .'
    'We're going to . . .'
    'I'm angry about . . .'

3. Maybe all you want to do is let it be known you disagree with what is going on, or with the way something was done or said. Write a letter-poem to a person you disagree with; eg President or Prime Minister of the USA, France, USSR, South Africa; your mum; a judge; a producer of a TV programme; a newspaper editor; a headmaster.

Here is a word that is behind a lot of fighting back –

Oppress, v.t. Overwhelm with superior weight or numbers or irresistible power; lie heavy on, weigh down (spirits, imagination, etc.); govern tyrannically, keep under by coercion, subject to continual cruelty or injustice, so **oppression**.

from *The Concise Oxford Dictionary*

People who believe they are oppressed do things that show their feelings towards the oppressor. Here are some examples:
punch them
send them a letter of complaint
draw a cartoon of them
make up a song about them
go and see a friend and talk about them
go and see an MP
write a letter to a paper
organise a meeting
refuse to do what the oppressor tells them to do
fight back

Fighting back in poetry can mean a variety of things:
— Describing the way the oppressed fights back
— Attacking the way the oppressor oppresses
— Mocking the oppressor
— Celebrating the lives of the oppressed
— Mourning, defeats, misfortunes and disasters of the oppressed
— Calling upon the oppressed to take action.

Much of this kind of poetry is despised, ignored, thought to be bad, hidden. It is almost as if the poetry of the oppressed, poetry about the oppressed, poetry about oppressors, is itself oppressed. Famous writers find that their fightback poems get ignored and left out of books (Shelley is just one example). And in fact poets have been imprisoned (eg Theodorakis, the Greek songwriter) or even killed (eg Victor Jara, the Chilean folk singer), because their words have been thought to be 'dangerous'. It is forbidden to even mention Victor Jara's name in Chile today.

GEORGE LINDO

George Lindo was arrested, charged and convicted for robbery with violence in Bradford. Many people demonstrated and petitioned, saying that he was innocent. Linton Kwesi Johnson wrote the following poem, as part of that campaign. Eventually, George Lindo was set free from prison and officially pardoned. Some of you reading the poem may not be familiar with some of the spellings and some of the words, so I've put a short glossary afterwards. Some of you will recognize it as the talking voice of Black British people whose parents or grandparents came from the West Indies.

IT DREAD INNA INGLAN

(for George Lindo)
dem frame-up George Lindo
up in Bradford Toun
but di Bradford Blacks
dem a rally roun

mi seh dem frame-up George Lindo
up in Bradford Toun
but di Bradford Blacks
dem a rally roun. . . .

Maggi Tatcha on di go
wid a racist show
but a she haffi go
kaw,
rite now
African
Asian
West Indian
an' Black British
stan firm inna Inglan
inna disya time yah
far noh matteh wat dey say,
come wat may,

we are here to stay
inna Inglan,
inna disya time yah. . . .

George Lindo
him is a working man
George Lindo
him is a family man
George Lindo
him nevah do no wrang
George Lindo
di innocent one
George Lindo
him noh carry no daggah
George Lindo
him is nat no rabbah
George Lindo
dem haffi let him go
George Lindo
dem bettah free him now!

LINTON KWESI JOHNSON

dem	– them
toun	– town
di	– the
roun	– round
mi seh	– me say – I say
wid	– with
haffi go	– has to go
kaw	– because
stan	– stand
inna Inglan	– in England
inna disya time yah	– in this time – now
far	– for
mattah	– matter
wat	– what
nevah	– never
daggah	– dagger
rabbah	–robber
bettah	– better

After Leaving the Castle

A woman who is married to a Lord, one day decides to run away with a band of gypsies. When her husband finds that she's gone, he rushes after her, pleads with her to return to him and the luxuries of his castle, but she refuses and says she prefers life with the gypsies.

That's the story of the Raggle Taggle Gypsies.

Liz Lochhead has written an alternative view. She tells the story of five nights (four nights and one day, actually) and what the woman does. By describing what she *does*, Liz Lochhead suggests what the lady thinks, and so we get an idea of how over five days the lady's views about her situation change.

AFTER LEAVING THE CASTLE

On the first night
the lady lay in the dark with her lover
awake all night
afraid her husband would pursue her.

On the second night
the lady lay awake in the arms of her lover
her tongue and teeth idly
exploring the cold of his earring.

On the third night
the lady lay awake afraid
her husband would never come after.

On the fourth night
the lady thought as she drifted off to sleep
how monotonous it would be
to live on rabbit stew forever
& she turned a little away
from snoring, the smell of wild garlic.

When they passed him on the road
on the fifth day,
she began to make eyes at the merchant.

LIZ LOCHHEAD

On the first night with her new lover, she is still living in terror that her husband is coming to find her. She is in love with one man and afraid of another. Why is she afraid? Will he capture her? beat her? kill her? kill her lover? We don't know, but it is a *weak* situation to be in. Her husband is dominating her even though he isn't there.

On the second night, she seems to have got rid of the dominating picture of her husband and is enjoying making love with her gypsy lover. She is relaxed – 'idly exploring the cold of his earring'.

On the third night, there is a new twist. She is worried that her husband does not care that she's upped and gone. She is worried he does not love her enough to bother to come and find her. The husband is still dominating her mind. She is still unfree.

On the fourth night, she seems to have done two things. Because he's not mentioned, she seems to have forgotten about the husband, she's neither afraid he's going to punish her, nor is she hurt that she has not succeeded in making him jealous or angry. Secondly, she is getting fed up with this new affair. The grub's dull, her lover snores and either he or the woodland undergrowth where they sleep stinks of garlic. The reality of wonderful runaway romances is wearing away the wonderful romance. Even lovers snore.

On the fifth day, her mind has changed completely. She has clearly put all concern for her husband behind her – she has broken free from him, but now she doesn't seem to care much for her gypsy lover – she seems anxious to hitch up with a new man:

'She began to make eyes at the merchant'.

I want to suggest two alternative trains of thought about this.

1. 'What a great woman!' She has learnt to free herself of guilt at leaving a man. She has freed herself of dependency on a man, because she no longer needs to make him jealous; instead of this weak, subservient, inferior state of mind, she is now independent, free and guiltless. She is a free agent and can make eyes at a man without waiting for men to make eyes at her. She is in control of herself and not held in control by a previous husband or lover.
2. 'What a silly woman!' She is a pathetic example of one of those women who is so dependent on men, that she isn't dominated simply by one man – a husband – but lets herself be dominated by *all* men. No sooner

does she get fed up with one man, she's off after another. She hasn't even the guts or self-will or belief in herself as an independent woman to live free of men. Instead, she can only escape one bad or boring relationship with a man by diving straight away into another one.

These judgements depend very much on who *we* are. What *we* think about women who can chase men as freely as men chase women. In our society, there is a great inequality between the sexes in our attitudes towards men who have several lovers and women who do the same. Men sometimes talk of those men who 'get off with' plenty of girls as if they're clever, brilliant, admirable. Girls who do the same are 'sluts' or 'scrubbers'; insults may even be hurled at girls who are 'unfaithful' or as 'promiscuous' as boys.

Liz Lochhead, I would guess, thinks this situation is wrong and therefore thinks that a woman who *is* free to choose her lovers without being panic-stricken about what a husband or the neighbours or other women think of her, is a *strong* woman – a woman who is an equal of men in her treatment of the opposite sex. To do this, she has had to learn how to treat men as they treat her.

ACTIVITY

1. Read *After Leaving the Castle* again and then answer these questions.
   (i) How does the woman change her attitude to men?
   (ii) Is she stronger or is she weaker at the end of the poem?
   (iii) **What do you think Liz Lochhead thinks of her?**
   (iv) Is this a fightback?
   (v) Is it a change for the worse, because she is now a 'fallen woman', or just a change from one kind of subservient position towards men to another?
2. Write a poem which retells a well-known love story from an alternative or unexpected point of view, eg 'Sleeping Beauty' or 'The Sound of Music' or 'Romeo and Juliet'.

Here is a poem by Adrian Mitchell, protesting about the possibility of a nuclear war. He takes as his starting point the kind of instructions given in government pamphlets which tell you what to do if a nuclear war started. Appendix IV describes the equipment you are advised to take into a nuclear fallout shelter.

'APPENDIX IV

REQUIREMENTS IN THE SHELTER

Clothing
Cooking Equipment
Food
Furniture
Hygiene
Lighting
Medical
Shrouds'

What?

'Shrouds.
Several large, strong, black plastic bags and a reel of 2-inch, or wider, adhesive tape can make adequate air-tight containers for deceased persons until the situation permits burial.'

No I will not put my lovely wife into a large strong black plastic bag
No I will not put my lovely children into large strong black plastic bags
No I will not put my lovely dog or my lovely cats into large strong black
   plastic bags

I will embrace them all until I am filled with their radiation

Then I will carry them, one by one,
Through the black landscape
And lay them gently at the concrete door
Of the concrete block
Where the colonels
And the chief detectives
And the MPs
And the Regional Commissioners
Are biding their time

And then I will lie down with my wife and children and my dog and my
   cats

and we will wait for the door to open

ADRIAN MITCHELL

IMAGINE

Imagine there's no heaven
It's easy if you try.
No hell below us,
Above us only sky.
Imagine all the people,
Living for today.

Imagine there's no countries
It isn't hard to do,
Nothing to kill or die for
And no religion too.
Imagine all the people
Living life in peace.
You may say I'm a dreamer,
But I'm not the only one.
I hope some day you'll join us
And the world will be as one.

Imagine no possessions
I wonder if you can
No need for greed or hunger
A brotherhood of man.
Imagine all the people
Sharing all the world
You may say I'm a dreamer,
But I'm not the only one.
I hope some day you'll join us
And the world will live as one.

JOHN LENNON

ACTIVITY

Choose one poem from this chapter and then answer these questions.
1. Who is fighting back?
2. What are they fighting against?
3. Has the poem changed your mind about anything?
4. Describe how and why it has changed your mind.
5. If you disagree with the 'fight', write down your arguments against it, as an essay or a poem.

IMAGES OF PLACE

Now you see it . . .

People sometimes ask 'What was your first impression of me when we met?' What they're asking is: 'What feelings did you have about me the very first time you saw me?' It can be the same with a place. If you walk down the street, along the canal, in the park – anywhere – you can ask yourself some questions. What can I see? What are my feelings about what I can see? Of course, all your other senses come into it as well: hearing, smell and touch.

I SAID:

I'll tell you what I did in town
I saw a greengrocer in the underground
with his pockets full of oranges,
a paperboy yawned
so you could see his tonsils,
there was one old football boot
lying in City Square
and round the island came the Odeon Commissionaire
riding on a moped with his uniform flying,
a hamster saw a parrot sneeze
the shop blinds flapped and an oil tanker squealed,
the peanut man
lost a bag beneath a bus's wheels
'Mind your peanuts', a girl shouted
his tray was slipping and a taxi hooted
'Oh help me then', he called out
I said: 'Where I'm sorry where?'
and forty thousand pigeons climbed into the air.

MICHAEL ROSEN

BIRKENHEAD

A dirty dark dusk floats comfortably,
reminding people of their misfortune in wartime,
reminding people of terror and fear,
of old and young,
and old Birkenhead and its ways.

Ilchester Square,
Alleyo 123.
You're caught.
    No I'm not.
Some playing jacks on the uneven paving stones.
The blocks of flats looked into an arena
where children played and fought with each other.
Line up at number 57 for flapjacks
with penny in hand, from Mrs Brown,
or borrow a bike off Mrs Button,
for a penny an hour.
Sometimes, hours of happiness,
other times, sadness in this rough area.
This is all gone,
but memories linger on.

The torment of the round arena,
tapping on windows, pulling tongues,
and then running away,
tripping over his undone shoe laces.
He pulled up his knee-length shorts
and snorted,
hitting small children and laughing.
The torment of the street,
he was frightened of no one,
the terror of the Bull Ring.

The old market.
The wind blows on the old shutters.
Once they were used,
heels clicking on the cobblestone floors.
Once there was an atmosphere.
Once everything there was alive.
Walking round an old building,

full of buyers and sellers.
The same old dirty smell,
memories of the past.
As you sit outside on the doorstep,
dressed in an old-fashioned outfit;
longing to smell the atmosphere.

Jessie Annie Hudson (1892 – 1972)
Rub, rub, scrub, scrub, splash, splash,
washing in the old dolly tub,
aching arms, through mangling clothes, never stop,
rubbing the step,
eating, working and play,
hanging out the washing with dolly pegs,
Sun shines through the small square windows,
working all the time.
Mam's work never done.

The Tip.
Concealed in old drums,
discarded tyres and wrecks of cars,
children lounge about over the rubbish;
anything to do in their spare time,
covered in muck and dust they play.
At night, the wasteland is empty,
only the moonlight shines.

Modern council houses with a cheap structure
stand gloomily,
leaning to one side.
The green grass once stretched over the land,
a gate led to each part,
altogether seven gates.
Now, the clean countryside spoilt,
by dirty, crowded houses and factories.
The light blue sky,
turns to a smoky grey,
silhouetting the plan of houses for the future.

JOANNE EDWARDS (AGE 12)

ACTIVITY

1. Write down some of the words and sayings and nicknames people have for places – or what they say when they complain about the bad state such and such a place has got into; or what they say when they see a place they admire, or place they're fond of. You can construct poems out of these sayings and nicknames or imitate the sound and style of them to make your own.
2. Think back to your first impressions of secondary school or a village, town or city. Jot down some phrases connected with these impressions. Then rearrange the phrases into a poem, adding any other words you like.

Nearly everywhere on this planet shows signs that men or women or both have been there. In the middle of the Atlantic Ocean the muck and rubbish thrown out of the ships floats on the water; you walk down your street and every step you take is on constructed and reconstructed concrete, cement, stone and tarmacadam. Everywhere you look there is something built, carved, processed, shaped, worn, planted, dumped, broken, cleaned by men, women or children.

You take a walk through a park, or some woods and even there the handiwork of planter, keepers, holiday-makers or gardeners can be seen. Many of the animals and plants are the way they are because of what human beings have done to the earth or the air. So, everywhere you look has a history; a background that is made by human beings – woman and man-made. This may seem obvious, but let's try something out.

Think of your house or flat. Do you know anything at all about who built it? How many people built it? How long it took them? When they did it? What sort of living they made out of building it? What kind of place they lived in while they were building your home? Most people don't know these answers.

Think of the biggest, grandest building in your area: Who built it? How many? How long? When? What sort of living? What kind of place did *they* live in?

Now take a look again at the schools, offices, shops, factories or farms in your area. Why are they *where* they are? Who decided to put them there? Who had to move to make way for what's there now? When was that done?

QUESTIONS FROM A WORKER WHO READS

Who built Thebes of the seven gates?
In the books you will find the names of kings.
Did the kings haul up the lumps of rock?
And Babylon, many times demolished
Who raised it up so many times? In what houses
Of gold-glittering Lima did the builders live?
Where, the evening that the Wall of China was finished
Did the masons go? Great Rome
Is full of triumphal arches. Who erected them? Over whom
Did the Caesars triumph? Had Byzantium, much praised in song
Only palaces for its inhabitants? Even in fabled Atlantis
The night the ocean engulfed it
The drowning still bawled for their slaves.

The young Alexander conquered India.
Was he alone?
Caesar beat the Gauls.
Did he not have even a cook with him?
Philip of Spain wept when his armada
Went down. Was he the only one to weep?
Frederick the Second won the Seven Years' War. Who
Else won it?

Every page a victory.
Who cooked the feast for the victors?
Every ten years a great man.
Who paid the bill?

So many reports.
So many questions.

BERTOLT BRECHT
(Translated by Michael Hamburger)

ACTIVITY

1. Ask yourself the simple questions on p. 74 about your house or school or a nearby building. Make notes of your answers, and then use the notes to make a poem about the place.
2. Pretend you are one of the builders, gardeners, cleaners of a place you know. Find out what kind of work it is (or was) to lay a brick, make a door, sweep a street, drive a crane, wash a window, etc. Write a short poem describing the work, from the point of view of one of those workers.
3. Pick somewhere – anywhere – and, armed with a notebook or a tape recorder, see whether you can find out the answers to any of the questions on p. 74. Sometimes the answers will come from a book, a newspaper, your mum or dad, grandparents, people doing a job, a 'guide' or a teacher.

Two images of dockland

This poem was written after walking out of the door of the George Green's School, London, and looking at a nearby building.

THE OLD WAREHOUSE

The windows are smashed,
They are making shapes with the cracks.
The wind bellows through the rubble
The pigeons are cooing as they sit on the bricks.
The feathers on their wings
Clatter away as I take one step.
The scruffy buildings are not in use,
So the pigeons have made an empire of their own,
Where the ruler sits in fear of humans
Marching through like the Romans on their
RAMPAGE!

DANNY MARRIOTT (AGE 15)

After Danny Marriott had written 'The Old Warehouse', he looked at pictures, read and listened to a few stories about things that happened in the past in exactly the same place. 'Chainman' was written after that small piece of research. It provides a very different image of the docks from his first poem. It is a poem about dockers waiting for work in 1890. They have to wait behind a chain, until called.

CHAINMAN

As the hinges start to creak
We push and push to turn the chain,
Just waiting to hear our name.
The ganger's in sight so they start to fight,
Only to work through the day.
My hat comes off as the man
Behind me raises his hand just to be called out.
The gangers go by,
My stomach is hurting as I'm pushing on the chain,
Just waiting to be called out.
I'm not called out.
I walk away while the beggar
Shouts 'My name is! My name is! My name is!

DANNY MARRIOTT (AGE 15)

ACTIVITY

1. Write about what you see when you walk out the door of your school and show what you *feel* about it. Set it out in a way you think will make people listen best.
2. Research about the things *you* saw in (1), and then write a poem about the same place one hundred years ago.

West India Dock, 1965

West India Dock, 1980

Behind the images

One of the most spectacular buildings in London is called Centre Point. It stands next to Tottenham Court Road Station at the junction of four famous streets, Charing Cross Road, Tottenham Court Road, Oxford Street and New Oxford Street. It is huge and white, standing high above the traffic in the street below.

Here are two ways of writing about this building. The first is the way the architect wrote about it in 1968 when it was built.

'Whatever you think of Centre Point, it belongs to the decade in which English youth finally asserted itself in supreme confidence above the mediocrity of the muddle-through, middle-of-the-road mentality. Like the Beatles, Mary Quant, this building expresses the supreme confidence of sheer professionalism. It has transcended its original role as a building and taken on a much wider social aspect. You may not like it, but you can't ignore it. More than any other building, Centre Point made London swing, it backed Britain, a product of real team work which must figure as an invisible export. Soaring to success. Master of all it surveys . . . Centre Point.'

COLONEL R. SEIFERT
in BUILDING, 24 MAY 1968

Ten years later, it was as empty as it was when it was first built.

At Centre Point there stands a tower,
Thirty storeys high or more
An office block with no-one there
Been empty now, nigh on ten years.

Near Lambeth Walk there's rows of houses,
Whole families crammed in one damp room.
How much'd it cost to build that b_____ ?
How much to give them decent homes?

When I look up at that fat tower,
I see the children of the slums.
When I stand at Centre Point, boy,
I think I hear the sound of drums.

JOHN POLE

Both pieces are about the same place; both pieces express opinions about this place. Both pieces summon up other people, other images, in order to comment on Centre Point.

Colonel Seifert, the architect, links the building with English youth, the Beatles, Mary Quant, swinging London, the Back Britain Campaign and a 'master'.

John Pole links the picture of Centre Point with another area of London, where there are slums and cramped living conditions. He makes two contrasts:
(i) all the empty space of one building and the cramped conditions of other buildings;
(ii) the money it cost to build Centre Point and the money it would cost to give people, who live in slums, decent homes.

Colonel Seifert's writing is a proud claim.
John Pole's poem is a complaint.
Colonel Seifert says Centre Point is a success.
John Pole says Centre Point is a crime.
Colonel Seifert seems almost to be selling Centre Point to us.
John Pole is attacking it.
Colonel Seifert sees a 'Master of all it surveys' (like an Emperor?)
John Pole sees 'the children of the slums'.
Colonel Seifert sees his building as a symbol of an exciting period of history.
John Pole sees it as representing something unfair and unequal in society.

ACTIVITY

1. Both writers about Centre Point are trying to convince, both describe and express opinions in their writing.
   Which of the two do you agree with?
2. Write about a building or place that you know in the way that Colonel Seifert or John Pole writes.

WAR POETRY

I don't suppose many of you reading this have ever been in a war. I haven't. For us, then, war poetry is a poetry that tells us about experiences that we ourselves haven't had. For instance, it can be an alternative way of finding out what it feels like to be in a war. We've seen films, read books, seen TV programmes, read comics and heard parents' and grandparents' stories, all giving their versions of war.

Richard Harris in 'The Wild Geese', Rank Organisation.

Can poetry do anything that films, books, TV programmes, comics, and parents' stories can't do? I'm not sure I know the answer to this question. It must be something to do with whatever it is that makes poetry special, or important, or unique.

Here is a group of poems written about the Second World War.

FIVE MINUTES AFTER THE AIR RAID

In Pilsen,
Twenty-six Station Road,
she climbed to the Third Floor
up stairs which were all that were left
of the whole house,
she opened her door
full on to the sky,
stood gaping over the edge.

For this was the place
the world ended.

Then
she locked up carefully
lest someone steal
Sirius
or Aldebaran
from her kitchen,
went back upstairs
and settled herself
to wait
for the house to rise again
and for her husband to rise from the ashes
and for her children's hands and feet to be stuck
    back in place.

In the morning they found her
still as stone,
sparrows pecking her hands.

MIROSLAV HOLUB

NAMING OF PARTS

Today we have naming of parts. Yesterday,
We had daily cleaning. And tomorrow morning
We shall have what to do after firing. But today,
Today we have naming of parts. Japonica
Glistens like coral in all of the neighbouring gardens,
    And to-day we have naming of parts.

This is the lower sling swivel. And this
Is the upper sling swivel, whose use you will see,
When you are given your slings. And this is the piling swivel,
Which in your case you have not got. The branches
Hold in the gardens their silent, eloquent gestures,
    Which in our case we have not got.

This is the safety-catch, which is always released
With an easy flick of the thumb. And please do not let me
See anyone using his finger. You can do it quite easy
If you have any strength in your thumb. The blossoms
Are fragile and motionless, never letting anyone see
    Any of them using their finger.

And this you can see is the bolt. The purpose of this
Is to open the breech, as you see. We can slide it
Rapidly backwards and forwards: we call this
Easing the spring. And rapidly backwards and forwards
The early bees are assaulting and fumbling the flowers;
    They call it easing the Spring.

They call it easing the Spring: it is perfectly easy
If you have any strength in your thumb: like the bolt,
And the breech, and the cocking-piece, and the point of balance,
Which in our case we have not got; and the almond-blossom
Silent in all of the gardens and the bees going backwards and
    forwards,
    For today we have naming of parts.

HENRY REED

SURVIVORS

With the ship burning in their eyes
The white faces float like refuse
In the darkness – the water screwing
Oily circles where the hot steel lies.

They clutch with fingers frozen into claws
The lifebelts thrown from a destroyer,
And see, between the future's doors
The gasping entrance of the sea.

Taken on board as many as lived, who
Had a mind left for living and the ocean,
They open eyes running with surf,
Heavy with the grey ghosts of explosion.

The meaning is not yet clear,
Where daybreak died in the smile –
And the mouth remained stiff
And grinning, stupid for a while.

But soon they joke, easy and warm,
As men will who have died once
Yet somehow were able to find their way –
Muttering about their food and pay.

Later, sleepless at night, the brain spinning
With cracked images, they won't forget
The confusion and the oily dead,
Nor yet the casual knack of living.

ALAN ROSS

You could see all those people on the deck before the ship was hit, and they were just standing there like ordinary people, and then you could see them sliding off the thing and then jumping into the sea . . . In the water you see people totally unreal; they're just within a minute of the end of their lives. And then suddenly they're out of the water and they realize that there's another life going to start, and they can't tell for a little while which life they're in, the one that's going or the one that's just beginning. . . . I think people want to live, but there's a moment beyond which they don't really care whether they live or not. Alan Ross

Henry Reed, Miroslav Holub and Alan Ross. Three men's views of situations they've seen and they've thought about.

They describe *scenes* and give us an account of their thoughts as they describe them. Probably most of them were written down after they had left the scene – so they are like memories. They are describing pictures in their head and discovering their feelings and opinions about those pictures as they write: trying to find words that can make those pictures come alive in our heads; trying to find words that can let us know their opinions and feelings.

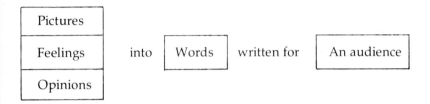

Sometimes this finding of words is quite a struggle. It isn't always very easy to find the words that will do the precise job you want them to do. In fact, people who write poems quite often

(i) use a word in a way no one has used it before
(ii) link one word to another in a way you have never heard before.

ACTIVITY

Pick out five unusual phrases from the poems on War, and then, in *each case* answer these questions:
1. What is the purpose of this piece of writing?
2. Does it help us understand things?
3. Do you think it gives you a better picture of things?

Alan Ross wrote a number of versions of the following poem *Night Patrol*. It is based on his experience as a naval officer on a destroyer during World War Two.

NIGHT PATROL

We sail at dusk. The red moon,
Rising in a paper lantern, sets fire
To the water; the black headland disappears,
Sullen in shadow, clenched like a paw.

The docks grow flat, rubbered with mist.
Cranes, like tall drunks, hang
Over the railway. The unloading of coal
Continues under blue arc-lights.

Turning south, the moon like a rouged face
Between masts, the knotted aerials swing
Taut against the horizon, the bag
Of sea crumpled in the spray-flecked blackness.

Towards midnight the cold stars, high
Over Europe, freeze on the sky,
Stigmata above the flickering lights
Of Holland. Flashes of gunfire

Lick out over meditative coastlines, betraying
The stillness. Taking up position, night falls
Exhausted about us. The wakes
Of gunboats sew the green dark with speed.

From Dunkirk red flames open fanwise
In spokes of light; like the rising moon
Setting fire to the sky, the remote
Image of death burns on the water.

The slow muffle of hours. Clouds grow visible.
Altering course the moon congeals on a new
Bearing. Northwards again, and Europe recedes
With the first sharp splinters of dawn.

The orange sky lies over the harbour,
Derricks and pylons like scarecrows
Black in the early light. And minesweepers
Pass us, moving out slowly to the North Sea.

ALAN ROSS

Alan Ross's poem does not tell us about any feelings. It is almost entirely *visual*. Night-lights. It is the *pictures* of the Night Patrol that convey his feelings. Night is, of course, dark, yet in each verse there is a picture of something light: eg 'red moon', 'blue arc-lights', 'flashes of gunfire', 'splinters of dawn',

In the first verse there are three events –
we sail at dusk
the moon rises
and *the headland disappears* out of sight.

We sail at dusk is described like that; no more, no less. It is what is often called a bald statement – which is itself a metaphor; after all a statement can't go bald – in very plain, direct, literal language. But the rest of this first verse is nearly all in language that expects us to imagine, *figurative language*.

The moon rises looking as if it were inside a paper lantern. Then it looks as if it *sets fire* to the water. It's red. And, in Alan Ross's mind, it looks like something alight – a paper lantern, so maybe the red moonlight on the sea's surface looked like fire.

The headland disappeared. It looked *sullen*. Sullen means sulky, taciturn, silent and grumpy. Have you ever been sullen? What did you do? Hang your head? Put your face out of sight? Maybe, Alan Ross sees the headland doing that sort of thing. Because it disappears out of sight into the darkness, it looks as if it is being grumpy, silent and taciturn.

There are no human beings, no animals and no plants in this poem. There are no conversations. It is a picture of the sea, the sky, the dark coastline, and the machines or lights of war. To me, this makes the idea of a night *watch* come very clear in my mind. The person on board who has to look out into the night and report what he *sees*. This night-watch is alone (not necessarily lonely) confronted by these lights and machines of war: docks, cranes, railways, unloading of coal under arc-lights, ship's masts and aerials, gunfire, gunboats, derricks, pylons and minesweepers.

There is one phrase in this poem that I see as the central point of the poem. It is the statement that Ross makes about the night – before the dawn arrives: 'the remote/Image of death burns on the water'. It isn't the night and the dark that suggest death (as some poets like to suggest; Shakespeare in *Macbeth* for example) but the lights.

Again, as someone who has never witnessed a war, this is something I had never really thought about till I read this poem. Lights at night in war time, instead of being hopeful, friendly things, are images of death. This I find menacing and scarey. It is ordinary to find the night scarey. In war it is not only night. It is the lights at night too.

One further thought. The aloneness, the implied isolated position of the night-watch, expresses a kind of helpless observer feeling to me. That is to say Alan Ross implies – he does not say directly, he is simply a watch – there is nothing he can say or do that can change what is happening in front of him. Yet, by writing about that situation of being a helpless observer, the writer at that moment stops being helpless. He becomes a communicator. He conveys the helplessness, the isolation to us and so makes contact with someone else.

Feeling alone and saying to someone that you feel alone are two very different things. The second suggests you are about to overcome feeling alone. This poem, I believe, has just such a reaching-out-to-someone-else feeling because it is such a precise cold image of someone alone and watching. For me, any situation that human beings are forced into that makes them have the feeling that they are helpless and alone is worth fighting against. I would like to think Alan Ross's highly personal expression of *that* feeling is itself a kind of fight *against* that feeling.

VERGISSMEINICHT*

Three weeks gone and the combatants gone,
returning over the nightmare ground
we found the place again, and found
the soldier sprawling in the sun.

The frowning barrel of his gun
overshadowing. As we came on
that day, he hit my tank with one
like the entry of a demon.

Look. Here in the gunpit spoil
the dishonoured picture of his girl
who has put: *Steffi. Vergissmeinicht*
in a copybook gothic script.

We see him almost with content
abased, and seeming to have paid
and mocked at by his own equipment
that's hard and good when he's decayed.

But she would weep to see today
how on his skin the swart flies move;
the dust upon the paper eye
and the burst stomach like a cave.

For here the lover and the killer are mingled
who had one body and one heart.
And death who had the soldier singled
has done the lover mortal hurt.

KEITH DOUGLAS

*Forget me not.

NO MORE HIROSHIMAS

At the station exit, my bundle in hand,
Early the winter afternoon's wet snow
Falls thinly round me, out of a crudded sun.
I had forgotten to remember where I was.
Looking about, I see it might be anywhere –
A station, a town like any other in Japan,
Ramshackle, muddy, noisy, drab; a cheerfully
Shallow permanence: peeling concrete, litter, 'Atomic
Lotion, for hair fall-out,' a flimsy department-store;
Racks and towers of neon, flashy over tiled and tilted waves
Of little roofs, shacks cascading lemons and persimmons,
Oranges and dark-red apples, shanties awash with rainbows
Of squid and octopus, shellfish, slabs of tuna, oysters, ice,
Ablaze with fans of soiled nude-picture books
Thumbed abstractedly by schoolboys, with second-hand looks.

The river remains unchanged, sad, refusing rehabilitation.
In this long, wide, empty official boulevard
The new trees are still small, the office blocks
Basely functional, the bridge a slick abstraction.
But the river remains unchanged, sad, refusing rehabilitation.

In the city centre, far from the station's lively squalor,
A kind of life goes on, in cinemas and hi-fi coffee bars,
In the shuffling racket of pin-table palaces and parlours,
The souvenir-shops piled with junk, kimonoed kewpie-dolls,
Models of the bombed Industry Promotion Hall, memorial ruin
Tricked out with glitter-frost and artificial pearls.

Set in an awful emptiness, the modern tourist hotel is trimmed
With jaded Christmas frippery, flatulent balloons; in the hall,
A giant dingy iced cake in the shape of a Cinderella coach.
The contemporary stairs are treacherous, the corridors
Deserted, my room an overheated morgue, the bar in darkness.
Punctually, the electric chimes ring out across the tidy waste
Their doleful public hymn – the tune unrecognizable, evangelist.

Here atomic peace is geared to meet the tourist trade.
Let it remain like this, for all the world to see,
Without nobility or loveliness, and dogged with shame
That is beyond all hope of indignation. Anger, too, is dead.
And why should memorials of what was far
From pleasant have the grace that helps us to forget?

In the dying afternoon, I wander dying round the Park of Peace.
It is right, this squat, dead place, with its left-over air
Of an abandoned International Trade and Tourist Fair.
The stunted trees are wrapped in straw against the cold.
The gardens are old, old women in blue bloomers, white aprons,
Survivors weeding the dead brown lawns around the Children's
    Monument.

A hideous pile, the Atomic Bomb Explosion Centre, freezing cold,
'Includes the Peace Tower, a museum containing
Atomic-melted slates and bricks, photos showing
What the Atomic Desert looked like, and other
Relics of the catastrophe.'

The other relics:
The ones that made me weep;
The bits of burnt clothing,
The stopped watches, the torn shirts.
The twisted buttons,
The stained and tattered vests and drawers,
The ripped kimonos and charred boots,
The white blouse polka-dotted with atomic rain, indelible,
The cotton summer pants the blasted boys crawled home in, to bleed
And slowly die.

Remember only these.
They are the memorials we need.

JAMES KIRKUP

The effect of one atomic bomb, Hiroshima, 6 August 1945

In this poem I take Kirkup's voice to be that of a journalist. The poem sounds a bit like a very carefully written newspaper article or TV reporter's talk as he takes us for a trip round Hiroshima.

James Kirkup does not conjure up pictures of Hiroshima to us by suggesting that what he sees or hears seems as if it is something else. His method is to describe things in a more direct way. The poem is virtually a list of things he observes on his trip to Hiroshima. One word links these lists. It is the most important idea/word in the poem. It is the theme of the poem: 'memorials'.

'I had forgotten to remember where I was.'
Kirkup is a traveller, a tourist to the city where the first atomic bomb was dropped at the end of World War Two. Why had he forgotten? The answer lies in section one – the first list of little scenes that conjure up the picture of Hiroshima today – *'a town like any other in Japan.'*

He then interrupts this picture – section two – with a picture of the river as *unchanged, sad, refusing rehabilitation.* But maybe because it is unchanged this will not jog his memory.

Section three – the word 'memorial' crops up. The pictures are again presented like a list, but by now we learn that some of the things Kirkup the tourist sees are reminders of the past event.

So there are differences between these lists. The significance of each is different. Moreover Kirkup writes critically. In place of an image-conjuring method he writes expressing an opinion of what he sees as he sees it. It is a very different way to make a vision highly personal. It is not so much the *language* that is personal (as in *Night Patrol*) but the opinion.

Look at this list of words: ramshackle, muddy, noisy, drab, shallow, flimsy, flashy, soiled, sad, basely, slick, squalor, racket, awful, jaded, flatulent, dingy, treacherous, deserted, overheated, dead, left-over, stunted, hideous, freezing cold. They are all used in list one, two, three, four, and six.

They obviously convey Kirkup's disgust and dislike of what he sees. He is condemning what he sees as he describes it. When he gets to list seven, he holds back from opinion-phrases, yet this is the list that makes him weep.

The list is unpleasant; the adjectives and phrases here are: burnt, stopped, torn, twisted, stained, tattered, ripped, charred, polka-dotted with atomic rain, indelible, blasted.

The words described are: clothing watches, shirts, buttons, vests, drawers, kimonos, boots, blouse, pants, boys. So, from a city-wide landscape of buildings, trade, so-called memorials, and tourism, Kirkup focusses on a few small things – the personal garments of individual dead or dying people.

'Remember only these' he says. That is – forget the rest.
'They are the memorials we need.'

Why do we *need* these memorials? The title of the poem is *No More Hiroshimas*. I take this to be a slogan – a demand – Let there be no more Hiroshimas! If there are to be no more Hiroshimas what *action* should we take? Kirkup tells us that one action we must take is to remember those clothes and those boys. By remembering the clothes, we might also remember the people who wore them. The condition of the clothes tells us something of the way in which the people were destroyed.

But isn't there another suggestion? We need to remember these awful relics so that we will make sure, one way or another, there will not be another Hiroshima. Do you agree with that? Do you think that by knowing about these things, you will try to make sure there won't be another Hiroshima? Can a poem about war have that power?

ACTIVITY

1. Read *Vergissmeinicht* again (see p. 91).
    (i) Write about the poem in terms of its theme, mood and style.
    (ii) Write a short poem about the same event from the viewpoint of *either* the girlfriend *or* the British soldier three weeks earlier.
2. Take any two poems in this chapter that deal with the horror of war, Then compare the ways in which that horror is conveyed.
